Illustrators
Mike Atkinson, Jim Dugdale, Ron Jobson, John Marshall,
Bernard Robinson, Frederick St. Ward,
Mike Saunders, David Wright

Copyright © MCMLXXXV, MCMLXXXVI by World International Publishing Limited.
First published in U.S.A. 1985, second printing 1986 by Exeter Books.
Distributed by Bookthrift.
Exeter is a trademark of Bookthrift Marketing, Inc.
Bookthrift is a registered trademark of Bookthrift Marketing, Inc.
New York, New York.
All rights reserved.
ISBN 0-671-07744-9
Printed in France.

The
CHILDREN'S FIRST
ENCYCLOPEDIA

Compiled by Michael Dempsey

Exeter Books

NEW YORK

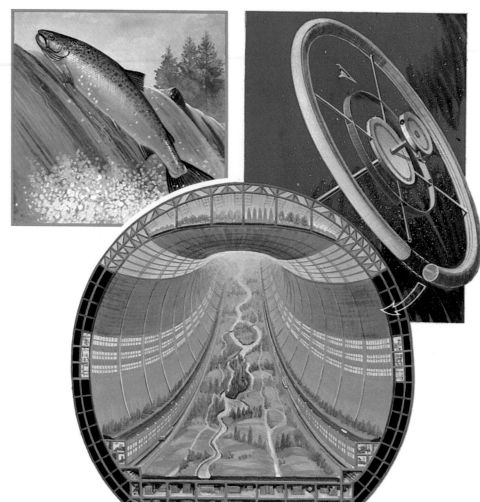

Contents

The Planet Earth

Our planet Earth is like a huge spaceship hurtling through space. It travels at over 62,000 mph around the Sun, completing an orbit in just over 365 days (one year). At the same time, along with the rest of the Solar System, it travels around the center of the Milky Way galaxy, taking about 200 million years to complete one of these vast journeys. The Earth also moves in a third way because it spins on its axis, making one turn every 24 hours (one day).

The Seasons

The axis is an imaginary line running through the center of the Earth, joining the North and South Poles. It is tilted by about $23\frac{1}{2}$ degrees from the upright. This means that as the Earth orbits the Sun, at certain times of the year the northern half of the Earth, or *northern hemisphere*, is tilted towards the Sun, and the *southern hemisphere* tilted away from it. As a result, the northern hemisphere gets more sunlight than the southern and so is warmer; it is summer in the north and winter in the south. At other times, the southern hemisphere is tilted towards the Sun and the northern hemisphere away from it; it is then summer in the south.

Below: An eclipse of the Sun occurs when the Moon is between the Sun and the Earth and a shadow of the Moon is cast onto the Earth's surface. The picture on the left shows a total eclipse of the Sun, with the Sun's atmosphere revealed.

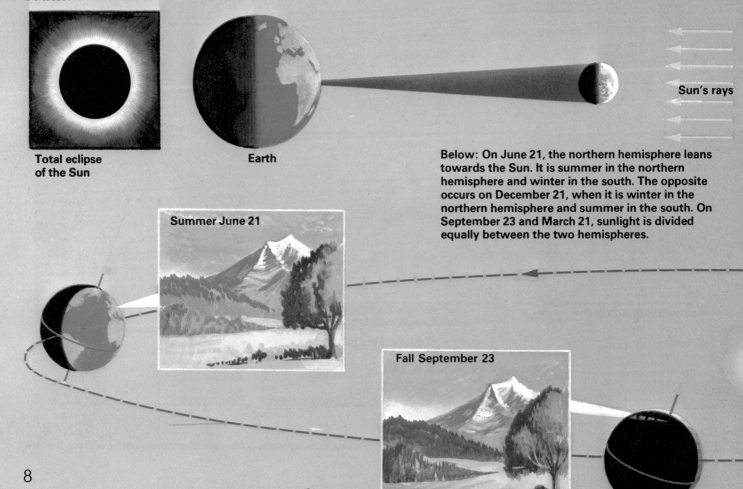

Sun's rays

Total eclipse of the Sun

Earth

Below: On June 21, the northern hemisphere leans towards the Sun. It is summer in the northern hemisphere and winter in the south. The opposite occurs on December 21, when it is winter in the northern hemisphere and summer in the south. On September 23 and March 21, sunlight is divided equally between the two hemispheres.

Summer June 21

Fall September 23

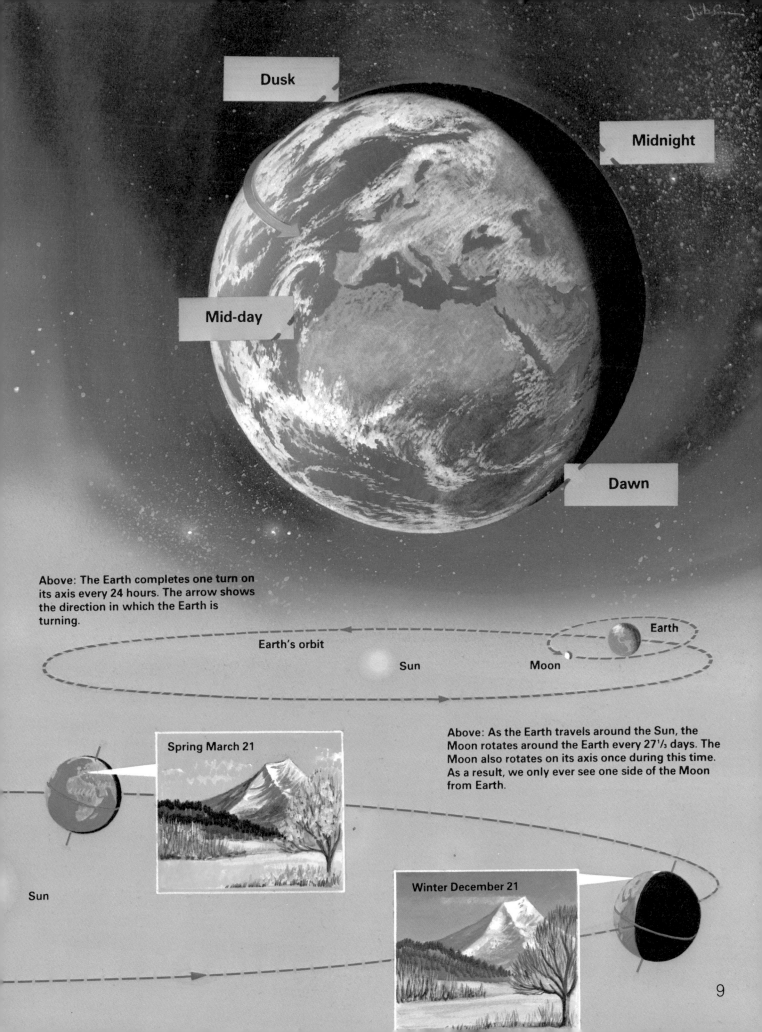

Dusk

Midnight

Mid-day

Dawn

Above: The Earth completes one turn on its axis every 24 hours. The arrow shows the direction in which the Earth is turning.

Earth

Earth's orbit

Sun

Moon

Above: As the Earth travels around the Sun, the Moon rotates around the Earth every 27$\frac{1}{3}$ days. The Moon also rotates on its axis once during this time. As a result, we only ever see one side of the Moon from Earth.

Spring March 21

Sun

Winter December 21

Sun   Mercury   Venus   Earth   Mars   Jupiter

10

POLAR CAPS ON MARS

Winter

Summer

Family of the Sun

Our Sun, like the millions of stars that twinkle in the night sky, is a glowing ball of hot gases. Nine planets, many of them with their own moons, orbit the Sun. The Earth is one such planet. Some planets, such as Earth and Mars, are rocky, while others, such as Jupiter and Saturn, are giant balls of gas. The Sun and the planets form the Solar System, along with asteroids (small, rocky bodies), comets (streams of dust and gas) and meteorites. Shooting stars are meteorites burning up as they enter the Earth's atmosphere.

Above: A view of Saturn from one of its seventeen sizeable moons, Tethys. Space probes have sent back much information about Saturn and its moons and rings. Above right: Mars has polar caps made of the frozen gas carbon dioxide. The caps melt in summer. Below: The Solar System.

Planet	Number of Moons	Distance from Sun, average in millions miles	Diameter (equator) in miles	Length of day	Length of year
Mercury	0	36	3,032	176 days	88 days
Venus	0	67	7,523	2,760 days	225 days
Earth	1	93	7,928	24 hours	365 days
Mars	2	142	4,222	24.6 hours	687 days
Jupiter	14?	484	88,750	9.8 hours	11.9 years
Saturn	17?	887	74,580	10.2 hours	29.5 years
Uranus	5	1,700	32,000	24 hours	84 years
Neptune	2	2,795	30,000	22 hours?	165 years
Pluto	1	3,667	2,000	6.4 hours	248 years

Saturn   Uranus   Neptune   Pluto

Exploring Space

Space shuttle

Above: Shuttle spacecraft are designed to take people and materials into space and then return to Earth. The materials will be used to build large space stations.

The Space Age began in 1957, when the Russians launched a satellite called Sputnik 1. Although it was little larger than a football, it was the first artificial satellite to orbit the Earth. This great achievement caused much rivalry between Russia and the USA. Both countries have had many successes. Russia was the first to send a man into space. The USA was the first to put people on the Moon. The work of these countries has greatly increased our knowledge of the Solar System. Research continues as space probes now reach out to the edge of the Solar System.

Life in Space

One of the aims of space research has been to discover whether life exists on other planets. We now know that there is no life on the Moon, which does not have any air. And so far, no proof has been found of life anywhere else in the Solar System, not even on our red neighbor, Mars. But scientists estimate that there are 130 solar systems in our part of the Milky Way galaxy. Some of these systems may contain planets much like the Earth. But the nearest star to the Sun is more than four light-years away. A light-year is over 6 million million miles. Four light-years is more than 3,000 times the distance across the Solar System.

The building of space stations has enabled much scientific work to be carried out. These stations have also shown that people can live in space without harmful effects. For example, two Russian cosmonauts spent 211 days in the Salyut 7 orbiting station in 1982 before returning to Earth. Their experience is helping designers to plan space colonies. These may one day house 10,000 or more people.

Viking space probe in orbit

Viking space probe releases landing craft

Landing craft descends, using a parachute and a rocket to ensure a soft landing

THE SPACE AGE

October 4, 1957: Russia launched Sputnik 1. It was the first Earth satellite.

1959: The Russian craft Luna 2 hit the Moon.

April 12, 1961: The Russian cosmonaut Yuri Gagarin orbited the Earth in Vostok 1. This was the first manned space flight.

1962: The first successful planetary probe, the American Mariner 2, passed near Venus.

1967: The Russian Venera 3 probe landed successfully on Venus.

1968: First manned flight of the American Apollo spacecraft around the Earth.

May 1969: First manned flight of the Apollo spacecraft around the Moon.

July 20, 1969: Neil Armstrong, commander of Apollo 11, and Edwin Aldrin, became the first men to walk on the Moon.

1969–72: Five more Moon landings were made by Apollo missions.

1973: The American Pioneer 10 took close-up pictures of Jupiter.

1974: The American Mariner 10 took close-up pictures of Mercury.

1975: An American and a Russian spacecraft linked up 140 miles above the Earth's surface.

1976: Two American Viking spacecraft landed on Mars.

1979–81: Voyager 1 and Voyager 2 sent back information about Jupiter and Saturn.

1981–82: Test flights of the US shuttle spacecraft Columbia.

Above: Viking space probes have been sent to Mars, a journey taking 10 months. After landing safely on the surface, the probes sent back pictures of the Red Planet. They searched for traces of life in the soil, but they did not find any proof of life on Mars.

ROUTE OF VOYAGER 2

July 1979 Jupiter

SUN   Earth

August 1981 Saturn

January 1986 Uranus

September 1989 Neptune

The diagram shows the route of the Voyager 2 spacecraft through the Solar System after its launch in August 1977. The figure of a man indicates the size of Voyager 2.

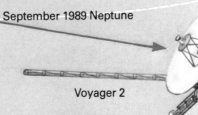

Voyager 2

Stars and Galaxies

Our Sun is one of 100,000 million stars in the Milky Way galaxy. Galaxies of stars are held together by gravity. Most galaxies are spiral in shape, like the Milky Way galaxy shown on the next page. The Milky Way galaxy measures 100,000 light years across, but it is only one of millions of galaxies in the Universe.

Scientists believe that stars form from clouds of hydrogen, other gases and dust. Gradually, gases are drawn towards the center, which becomes hot and glows. Nuclear reactions, caused when hydrogen is changed into another gas, helium, create enormous energy. Soon a new star is born, with a surface temperature of over 10000°F. Our Sun is a medium-sized star. Its diameter is 870,000 miles, 109 times the size of Earth.

Death of a Star

Stars last many millions of years, but eventually the hydrogen supply runs down, and the core of helium starts to collapse. This causes great heating and the outer parts of the star swell up like a balloon, creating a red giant star. When our Sun becomes a red giant, it will swallow up Mercury and Venus, and possibly Earth too. But this will not happen for 5,000 million years. At last, the red giant shrinks to become an Earth-sized, cold, white dwarf star.

CONSTELLATIONS: KEY

Northern Hemisphere
1 Pegasus, Flying Horse
2 Cygnus, Swan
3 Hercules, Kneeling Giant
4 Boötes, Herdsman
5 Ursa Major, Great Bear
6 Leo, Lion
7 Gemini, Twins
8 Orion, Hunter
9 Perseus, Champion
10 Polaris, Pole Star
11 Ursa Minor, Little Bear

Southern Hemisphere
12 Cetus, Sea Monster
13 Orion, Hunter
14 Lepus, Hare
15 Vela, Sails
16 Crater, Cup
17 Crux, Southern Cross
18 Lupus, Wolf
19 Scorpio, Scorpion
20 Sagittarius, Archer
21 Capricornus, Sea Goat
22 Phoenix, Phoenix

Below: Star charts of the northern hemisphere, left, and the southern hemisphere, right, show star constellations. There are 88 constellations in all. They are named after people, animals and objects and each has a Latin and an English name. (See key, right.)

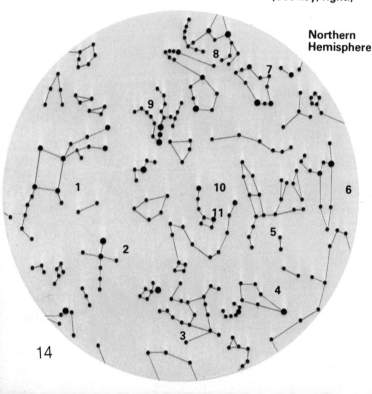

Northern Hemisphere

Southern Hemisphere

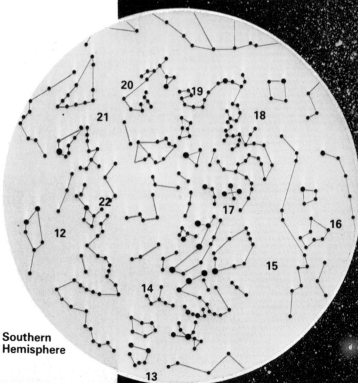

Top: The arrow shows our Sun, which is about two-thirds of the way from the centre of the Milky Way galaxy.
Above: The Crab nebula is the remains of an extremely big star which has blown up to create a glowing mass called a supernova.

The large diagram shows the life of a medium-sized star. Near the top of the page, a star forms from a cloud of gas and dust. The arrow shows the present state of our Sun. After millions of years, the star swells up to form a red giant, right. Much material is lost to space. The core then shrinks into a white dwarf star, below.

Beneath the Ground . . .

The Earth is about 8000 miles across, but the rocks which form the Earth's crust are rarely more than 40 miles thick. They rest on the denser (heavier) rocks of the *mantle* which surround the *core* of the Earth.

The crust is divided into large, rigid sections, called plates. These plates move around because of movements in the rocks beneath them. Hot, semi-liquid rocks rise up in the mantle and spread out sideways beneath the crust. Eventually, they cool and sink. The sideways currents of molten rock drag plates around like giant rafts. The plates move slowly, by only a few inches a year, but over millions of years they rip continents apart. As the plates move apart hot magma wells up and plugs the gap, then cools to form new rock.

The Changing Earth

About 180 million years ago all the continents were joined together in a vast supercontinent called Pangaea. This supercontinent then broke apart; North America split away from Europe, and South America drifted away from Africa. On a map these continents look as though they might fit together like pieces in a jigsaw. Continental drift, as this movement is known, continues today.

INSIDE THE EARTH

Crust: A thin crust encloses the Earth. The thickest parts of the crust are in the continents, under high mountain ranges. Here, the crust is up to 40 miles thick. But under the oceans, it averages only 4 miles in thickness.

Mantle: The mantle, under the crust, is about 1,800 miles thick. Here the rocks are denser than in the crust. Parts of the top of the mantle are molten.

Core: The Earth's core is about 4,300 miles across. It consists of two parts: the outer core is molten; the inner core solid.

Mantle — Inner core

Outer core

Crust

In places in the Earth's crust, two moving plates push against each other. One plate is then pushed beneath the other. The edge of the descending plate is melted and this molten rock supplies nearby volcanoes. Sometimes, colliding plates squeeze up crustal rocks between them into mountain ranges, like the Himalayas or the Alps.

Some plates slide alongside each other. For example, the San Andreas Fault in California is a plate edge. Plate movements are not smooth, because the plate edges are jagged and become jammed together. Tension makes them move against each other jerkily. These movements cause most of the world's worst earthquakes.

Ocean ridge

Ocean

Crustal plate

Ocean trench

Volcano

Magma rising to form new crustal rock

Magma forms as plate edge descends

Continent

Crustal plate

Above: The Earth's crust is split into sections called plates. These plates drift around because of movements in the partly fluid upper mantle. At ocean ridges, the oceans are being widened and new crustal rock is forming. The edges of some plates are pushed under others along ocean trenches. The plate edge melts to form magma, which rises through volcanoes.

. . Under the Sea

Around most continents are shallow seas which cover gently sloping areas called continental shelves. High parts of these shelves break through the water's surface to form islands. The continental shelves end at the steep continental slopes, and it is the tops of these slopes, not the coastlines, which are the real edges of the continents.

The continental slopes plunge down to the mysterious abyss. This includes large plains, mountain ranges (ocean ridges), volcanoes and ocean trenches. The deepest part of the oceans, 36,000 feet below the surface, is in the Marianas trench in the Pacific Ocean.

Continental shelf

Continental slope

Abyss

Right: Scientists study the dark ocean deeps in vessels called bathyscaphes. They have found fishes living in the deepest ocean trenches.

Ocean trench

The Violent Earth

In November 1963 a new island rose out of the sea off the coast of Iceland. This island, called Sertsey, is a volcano which began life on the ocean floor. Lava poured out of a *vent* (hole) in the Earth's crust and, as it cooled, gradually built up to form the massive cone which finally emerged as an island.

Lava comes from huge pockets of molten rock (magma) which form far below the surface of the Earth. When volcanoes erupt they are said to be *active*. Some spout columns of black ash high into the air; others pour blazing lava down their slopes in great streams. People living on the slopes must abandon their homes as fast as possible before they are buried under hot ash and lava. But after a volcano has stopped erupting and becomes *dormant* (sleeping), the people often return. This is because lava and ash make rich soils which are good for farming.

Earthquakes

Earthquakes are caused by many things, including volcanic eruptions. But most occur when rocks move against each other along great cracks in the Earth's crust. One such fault in California, the San Andreas Fault, is 600 miles long. In 1906 it caused a devastating earthquake when the rocks along its length slipped by over 20 feet. The buildings in San

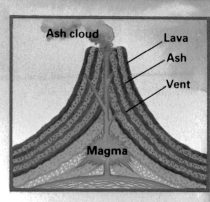

Volcanoes may explode with great force. Many volcanic mountains contain layers of lava and fine ash, as shown above. When volcanoes erupt, right, the ash may burn nearby forests and bury towns. Many volcanoes emit streams of lava. Lava may flow great distances. It destroys all living things in its path. Large lumps of molten rock hurled into the air are called volcanic bombs.

Below: Most waves at sea are caused by strong winds. But *tsunamis* are the result of earthquakes or volcanic eruptions on the sea bed.

Volcanic ash

Lava

Volcanic bombs

Tornadoes are destructive storms. They are whirlwinds and are common in the south-central United States. They are only about 440 yards across, but they can lift people and animals into the air and make buildings collapse. In 1925 a tornado in the USA killed 689 people in only three hours.

Francisco swayed and collapsed, and fires soon raged through the city.

Earthquakes on the ocean floor cause disturbances in the water which can create huge waves. Known as tidal waves, or *tsunamis* (the Japanese name), they crash over nearby coasts and cause great havoc.

Tornadoes and Hurricanes

Fierce storms can also be devastating. One violent storm is a whirlwind called a tornado. Torandoes are small in size, but fast winds in the center of the tornado leave a trail of destruction. Other large storms are called hurricanes, typhoons or tropical cyclones. They form over the oceans and move towards the land. Howling winds drive waves on to the land which, combined with heavy rain, flood coastal areas, drowning people and animals.

Composition of the air

Nitrogen (78.09%)

Oxygen (20.95%)

Other gases (0.03%)

Argon (0.93%)

Scale

Air pressure

Air pressure

Sun, Wind and Rain

Air is invisible, but we can weigh it in a laboratory. This is done by weighing an open jar and then weighing it again after we have pumped out the air. The difference between the measurements is the weight of the air in the jar. Roughly, the air in a drinking glass weighs about the same as an aspirin tablet.

The belt of air around the Earth is called the atmosphere. More than 99 per cent of the air is within 25 miles of the surface. The chief gases in the air are nitrogen and oxygen. There are small amounts of carbon dioxide, which plants absorb, and tiny amounts of ozone. Ozone is important because it blocks out most of the Sun's harmful ultraviolet rays. The air also contains invisible water vapour formed when the Sun's heat evaporates water from the Earth.

The atmosphere is always moving. At the equator, the Sun's rays heat the air, which causes it to rise. This creates a

Top: Diagram to show the various amounts of gases in the air. Above: A simple barometer, a device used to measure air pressure. Air presses down on water in a basin which forces water up the tube. As the air pressure changes, so the level of the water moves up or down against the scale. Above left: To illustrate the effect of air pressure, put a card over a glass of water and upend the glass. Air pressure will hold the card in place and stop the water escaping.

Below: The water cycle provides the land with a regular supply of fresh water. The Sun evaporates water from the oceans. This condenses into clouds which bring rain to the land. Rivers carry the water back to the oceans.

VARIOUS CLOUD TYPES

Cirrus

Cirrostratus

Cirrocumulus

Altostratus

Altocumulus

Stratocumulus

Cumulonimbus

Cumulus

Stratus

Nimbostratus

Precipitation: the water falls from the clouds to the land as rain

The water vapour condenses to form clouds

Transpiration: water is given off by trees and other plants

Evaporation from lakes and rivers

Water seeps into the ground and flows downhill towards the sea

20

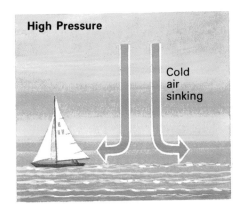

High Pressure

Cold air sinking

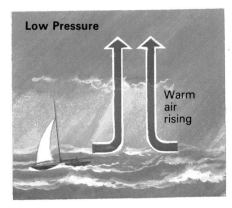

Low Pressure

Warm air rising

Snowflakes

zone of low air pressure, called the *doldrums*. The rising air eventually cools and spreads out north and south. It sinks back to Earth in the *horse latitudes* (around 30° north and 30° south). Because the air is sinking, these are zones of high air pressure. From these zones, some air flows back to the equator in the trade winds, and some flows polewards as the westerly winds.

The westerly winds meet up with cold easterly winds blowing from the poles. Depressions, which bring changeable, rainy weather, form in areas where the warm and cold air meet. Rain forms when air cools and water vapor condenses (liquefies) into tiny droplets. In temperate regions, exremely cold water droplets in clouds freeze around ice crystals. Finally, heavy crystals fall and melt to become raindrops. But if the air is cold, they fall as snow.

Left: On sunny days, the Sun heats the surface of the Earth, which warms up the lower layers of air. The warm air rises, carrying with it much invisible water vapor. As the air rises, it cools. Cool air cannot hold as much water vapor as warm air, and so some water vapor condenses into visible water droplets or ice crystals. These particles are so small that they stay suspended in the air and form clouds. If the upward air currents are strong, the clouds grow in size into huge cumulonimbus, or thunderstorm, clouds. In these clouds, the droplets and crystals collide and grow in size. When they are heavy enough, they fall as raindrops. But if the air near the ground is cold, they fall as snowflakes (above).

In regions where the air is sinking, far left, the air pressure is high. This happens in the horse latitudes, where the air gets warmer as it descends. Regions of high air pressure are associated with fine, stable weather and cloudless skies.

Right: At the equator the Sun's rays heat a far smaller area than at the poles, where the rays hit the Earth's surface at an angle. For this reason the heating is greatest at the equator. Here, the hot air rises and spreads out north and south, sinking back to Earth around the horse latitudes. At the surface, some air flows back towards the equator in the trade winds; some flows polewards in the westerly winds. Cold easterly winds blow from the poles.

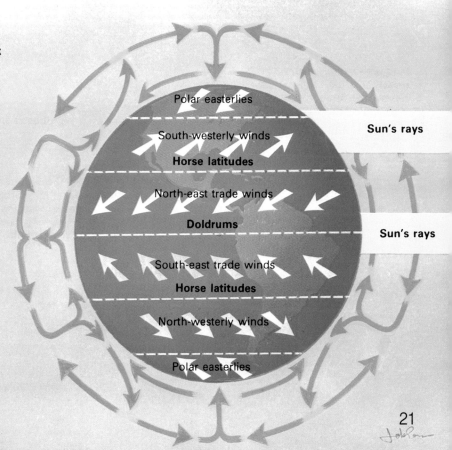

The Sun's heat causes water to evaporate from the oceans

Water flows into the sea by land and river to complete the cycle

Polar easterlies

South-westerly winds

Horse latitudes

North-east trade winds

Doldrums

South-east trade winds

Horse latitudes

North-westerly winds

Polar easterlies

Sun's rays

Sun's rays

21

Animal Lives

There are well over one million different kinds of animals, and they live on almost every part of the Earth's surface. There is animal life in caves, in deserts, and in the deep oceans. Only the frozen wastes of Antarctica and the highest and bleakest mountains are without animals – and even then, a few insects and spiders manage to exist on the coast of Antarctica, while swifts have been seen flying not far from the top of the world's highest mountain, Everest.

Naming Animals

Animals are often grouped together according to their similarities. This is known as classification. For example, some animals live in water, some on land; some are meat-eaters, some eat plants, and some eat both. Zoologists, the people who study animals, classify them according to the structure of their bodies. The simplest scientific group is the *species*, animals that are basically alike and breed among themselves. Similar species are grouped in *genera* (singular *genus*), genera are grouped in *families*, families in *orders*, orders in *classes*, and classes in *phyla* (singular *phylum*). All the phyla together make up the animal kingdom. Every group, from species to phylum, has a Latin name. In this way zoologists can give a name to every different kind, even those which share the same common name: for example, there are 4,000 species called hoverflies!

Butterfly (adult)

Caterpillar

Frog

Two types of metamorphosis. A butterfly (left) goes through four stages of development: egg, caterpillar, pupa, and adult. A frog's eggs (below) hatch first into limbless, long-tailed tadpoles. The tadpoles gradually grow legs and turn into frogs.

Eggs

Pupa

Eggs (frogspawn)

Tadpoles

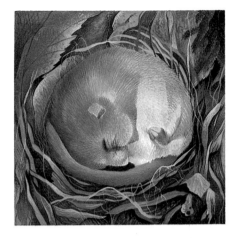

Top left: The cuckoo lays its egg in another bird's nest. The foster bird rears the cuckoo chick, which pushes the other chicks out of the nest.

Top centre: Some species of fish look after their eggs by carrying them around in their mouths until they hatch – and the very young fish also shelter in their mother's mouth.

Top right: When the weather is cold and food is scarce, animals such as the dormouse go into a deep, trance-like sleep, known as *hibernation*.

Left: Deer live in herds. They are usually peaceful animals, but during the rutting (mating) season the males fight each other for possession of the females, clashing their antlers together in fierce combat.

CHANGING SHAPE

Some animals go through a series of changes in shape before they become adults. This process is known as *metamorphosis*, from two Greek words meaning 'change of body'.

Butterflies and many other kinds of insects undergo a four-stage process. The insect starts life as an egg, and hatches into a larva (the larva of a butterfly is called a caterpillar). It spends a large part of its life as a larva, then shuts itself up in a case called a pupa, which it makes of silk. In the pupal stage the insect's body changes tremendously. Eventually it emerges as an adult.

Some insects, such as dragonflies, go through three stages: egg, nymph and adult. The nymph is similar to the adult and grows in size without changing shape.

Animals and Their Young

Wild animals have just two objectives in life: getting enough to eat, and finding a mate and breeding. Most animals move about for these purposes, though a few, such as corals, spend most of their lives fixed in one spot, filtering their food from the water in which they live.

All animals reproduce themselves. Some of the very simplest creatures, called protozoa, just divide to make two 'daughter cells'. Sponges throw out buds, which break off to form new individuals. But most animals reproduce sexually, by the mating of a male and a female. A female produces cells called eggs, and a male produces cells called sperm. When one of each kind of cell comes together they unite, and a new individual grows.

Many animals, including most fish and insects, never see their young. They lay and fertilize their eggs, and then leave them. Other animals look after their young until they are old enough to fend for themselves.

Animals of Long Ago

Animals have lived on Earth for millions of years. Scientists know about them because their remains are found embedded in rocks, turned to stone. These stony remains are called *fossils*.

Nobody knows exactly when life first appeared, because there are very few fossils older than about 570 million years, the start of what is called the *Palaeozoic Era*. Palaeozoic comes from Greek words meaning 'old life'. Scientists can put approximate dates to fossils because they can work out the age of the rocks in which they are found. Fossils show how plants and animals have changed, or evolved, throughout the Earth's long history.

The Pageant of Life

The first animals were *invertebrates*, animals that have no backbones, and they lived in the sea. They were soft, primitive creatures, rather like the jellyfish and sponges of today. The first animals with backbones – *vertebrates* – appeared about 450 million years ago. They were primitive forms of fish. After a long time some fish became able to breathe air and developed lungs (there are still some lungfishes today). From them came the first animals that could live both on land and in water. These *amphibians* were the ancestors of present-day frogs. They lived about 350 million years ago.

Many kinds of life evolved on land, including insects and reptiles. By about 200 million years ago giant reptiles, the dinosaurs, ruled the Earth. They died out suddenly, about 65 million years ago. By then birds and mammals had evolved, and mammals became the dominant animals. Man is one of the most recent mammals to evolve. Our ancestors appeared about two million years ago.

Below: Some of the dinosaurs, the giant reptiles which dominated the Earth for millions of years. Alamosaurus was one of several huge beasts feeding only on plants, while Tyrannosaurus was a fierce, meat-eating predator. By contrast, Compsognathus was about the size of a turkey. Archaeopteryx was the first known bird.

Tyrannosaurus

Compsognathus

Below: A panorama of life through prehistoric time, from the first forms of life in the sea, through the age of the dinosaurs, to the present-day age of mammals.

PALAEOZOIC ERA 570–230 million years ago

FOSSIL FORMATION

1

2

3

4

Left: How a fossil skeleton is formed:
1. a dead reptile sinks to the sea bed; 2. its body decays, and mud covers the skeleton; 3. the mud and the skeleton slowly harden to rock; 4. the sea bed rises through Earth movements, and the rock is worn away, revealing the fossil.

Alamosaurus

Archaeopteryx

Triceratops

Scolasaurus

MESOZOIC ERA 230–65 million years ago

CENOZOIC ERA 65 million years ago to present

The Insect World

Insects are found everywhere except in the open sea and the frozen Poles. There are more different species of insects than all the other animals put together. About a million have been identified, and more are being found all the time. They vary in size from fairy-flies just 1/100 inch long to stick insects 13 inches long and bulky Goliath beetles which weigh 3½ ounces.

Insects can always find somewhere to live and something to eat. Insects live in ponds and streams, in caves, up mountains and in deserts. Almost every kind of plant and animal substance has an insect that feeds on it. Insects play an important part in disposing of dead plants and animals, so that the substances of which these are made are returned to the soil to feed new plants. Many insects are essential for plants, anyway, because they pollinate them. They transfer pollen from one flower to another so that seeds will form from which new plants can grow.

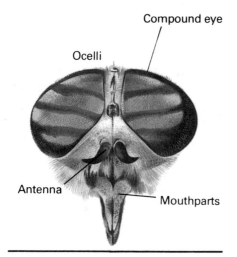

Compound eye

Ocelli

Antenna

Mouthparts

SEEING ALL AROUND

Insects cannot move their eyes to see around them. But to make up for this most species have two large *compound eyes*. Each compound eye has from 6 to 30,000 tiny lenses, depending on the species, and each lens is set at a slightly different angle. This gives the insect a wide field of vision. In addition many adult insects also have three simple eyes, called *ocelli*. The simple eyes can only detect light and dark. A typical insect's head, above, shows the two kinds of eyes, and also the antennae, or feelers, and the mouthparts, for chewing or sucking.

All Kinds of Insects

Entomologists – people who study insects – group the million or so different species into 29 main orders, according to the classification described on page 22. These orders are listed at the top of the facing page. So little is known about some of these orders that the insects in them have no common name, only a Latin one.

Although insects vary so much in shape and size, they all have the

Above: Ants foraging for food lay down a scent trail. This enables them to find their way back to the nest, and also guides other ants to the source of food. Like bees, wasps and termites, ants are social insects, with three castes: queen, males, and workers, who are female.

Honeybees

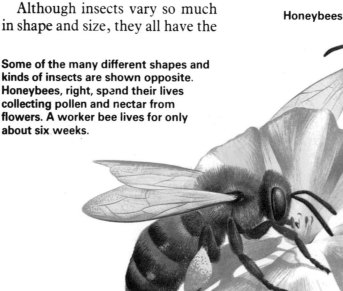

Some of the many different shapes and kinds of insects are shown opposite. Honeybees, right, spend their lives collecting pollen and nectar from flowers. A worker bee lives for only about six weeks.

THE 29 DIFFERENT GROUPS OF INSECTS

WINGLESS INSECTS
Silverfish (Thysanura)
Two-pronged bristletails (Diplura)
Protura (tiny soil dwellers with
    no common name)
Springtails (Collembola)

INSECTS WITH WINGS
A: With three-stage metamorphosis
Mayflies (Ephemeroptera)
Dragonflies (Odonata)
Stoneflies (Plecoptera)
Grylloblattodea (soil-dwellers
    with no common name)
Grasshoppers (Orthoptera)
Stick insects (Phasmida)
Earwigs (Dermaptera)
Web-spinners (Embioptera)
Cockroaches (Dictyoptera)

Termites (Isoptera)
Zoraptera (tropical insects with
    no common name)
Booklice (Psocoptera)
Biting lice (Mallophaga)
Sucking lice (Anoplura)
True bugs (Hemiptera)
Thrips (Thysanoptera)

B: With four-stage metamorphosis
Lacewings (Neuroptera)
Scorpionflies (Mecoptera)
Butterflies, moths (Lepidoptera)
Caddis flies (Trichoptera)
True flies (Diptera)
Fleas (Siphonaptera)
Bees, wasps, ants (Hymenoptera)
Beetles (Coleoptera)
Twisted-wing parasites
    (Strepsiptera)

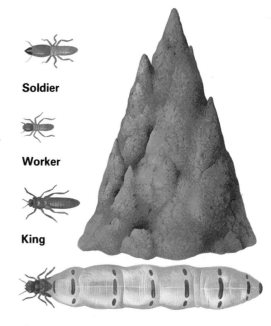

Soldier

Worker

King

Queen

Termites have a more elaborate caste system than ants, and build more elaborate nests – some termite mounds are 20 feet or more high. The termite castes are queen; king, who lives with her; workers, male and female, and soldiers. Queens and kings live a very long time, anything from 15 to 100 years.

same basic structure. The body of a typical insect is in three parts, the head, thorax and abdomen. These three parts show up very clearly in a wasp, for example. All insects have six legs, though the larvae of some, such as caterpillars, have extra legs while they are young. Nearly all adult insects have wings, and can fly.

Insect ways of life vary enormously. Mayflies, dragonflies and caddis flies are among those which spend most of their lives in the water, emerging for just a brief life in the air as adults. Ants, bees, wasps and termites are social insects, living in big, well-organized colonies, and working together.

Many insects are parasites, living on other animals. The best known are fleas and lice, but there are also many kinds of tiny parasitic wasps. Aphids and other true bugs suck the juices from plants. Most insects lay their eggs and forget about them, but some, such as bees and earwigs, look after their young.

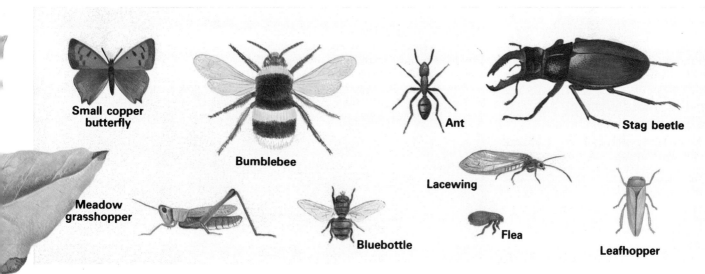

Small copper butterfly

Bumblebee

Ant

Stag beetle

Lacewing

Meadow grasshopper

Bluebottle

Flea

Leafhopper

The Seashore

The seashore is a place of violent contrasts. Plants and animals living there are under water for part of the time, and exposed to air, with possibly fierce winds or sizzling sunshine, the rest of the time. They may also be battered by heavy waves.

Over millions of years, living things on the shore have adapted to these harsh conditions. The only plants that can survive on the shore are seaweeds. Seaweeds are a form of algae, simple plants related to the green scum often seen on ponds. Although some appear to have stems and leaves, these features are merely divisions of the main body.

The shore-living animals have various methods of defense against waves and sunshine. Some burrow deep into the sand or mud. Others have hard shells, and cling to rocks. Soft-bodied animals such as sea anemones shelter in clefts under rocks.

Life Along the Shore

There are three main kinds of seashore: rock, sand or mud, and shingle. Some stretches of beach have all three kinds of shore. Muddy shores are often found in or close to river mouths. Nothing can live on shingle beaches, because when the waves crash on shore they roll the stones to and fro, grinding everything up. For this reason, it is rare to find an unbroken shell on shingle.

Rocky shores are the home of seaweeds, which are not found on sand or mud. There are three main kinds of seaweed: green, brown and red. The colors vary, and some browns are a greenish shade, while many reds look brown. Small animals take shelter under seaweed from the drying effect of sun and wind.

Molluscs, related to garden snails and slugs, are among the main animals on rocky shores. Some, such as sea snails and limpets, have only one shell. Others, such as mussels, have a pair of shells, called valves, hinged together.

THE THREAT TO THE BEACHES

The biggest threat to life on the seashore is not the heat of the Sun, the drying wind, or the blows of the waves, but pollution made by Man. Every year tons of debris are washed on shore, especially near busy sea lanes such as the English Channel. This includes old plastic containers and other waste matter thrown overboard from passing ships. Sometimes deck cargo is carried away in a storm, and this can include drums of poisonous or otherwise harmful chemicals.

An even bigger threat is posed by oil, spilled from ships, and especially from wrecked tankers. The oil coats all animals with which it comes in contact, and kills them.

From the land, sewage is pumped into the sea, and sometimes the tides bring it back on to the shore.

Fortunately, countries are now passing laws to try to keep the sea, and the shore, clean.

Below: Some of the many animals to be found in and around a rock pool. There are several different kinds of seaweed: bladderwrack has little bubbles of air along its fronds, which help it to float.

Cormorant

Limpet

Dog-whelk

Common starfish

Sea anemone

Hermit crab

Rock goby

Sea anemone

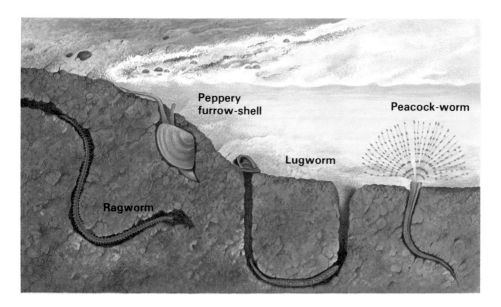

Peppery furrow-shell

Peacock-worm

Lugworm

Ragworm

Left: When the tide is in on a sandy beach, animals such as the peacock-worm come out of their burrows and open up. But, when the tide is out, they and the other burrowers stay firmly underground.

Below: Some of the many shells to be found on the beach. Some, such as the scallop, swim freely in the water near the shore, and live specimens are rarely washed up or left at low tide.

Many rocks are thickly covered in barnacles. They are related to crabs, which are also found on rocky shores, and on sand, too. There are often pools among the rocks, which never dry out. All these animals live in rock pools, along with soft-bodied creatures such as sea anemones.

More molluscs live on sandy shores, but they burrow deep into the sand and are not easy to find. They include tellins, razorshells, carpetshells and cockles. Also hidden under the sand are many kinds of worms, including lugworms, ragworms and peacock-worms.

Queen scallop

Keyhole limpet

Grooved razor shell

Edible cockle

Edible periwinkle

Pelican's-foot shell

Tower shell

Thin tellin

Common whelk

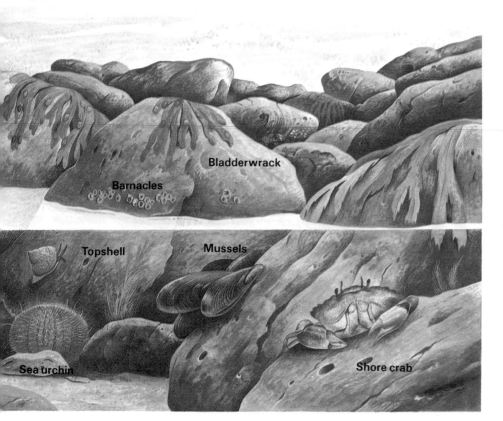

Bladderwrack

Barnacles

Topshell

Mussels

Sea urchin

Shore crab

Streams and Ponds

Plants and animals in streams and ponds have a very different kind of life from those on the seashore. For one thing the water is fresh. For another, the water level, though it may change according to how much rain has fallen, is much more constant than on the seashore. The plants and animals are also much more closely linked to the land around them.

Some ponds are small and shallow, and their waters are more or less stagnant. Others are deep lakes. Some are constantly enriched by material that is washed into them from streams. Plants grow in shallow mud, especially around the edges of ponds. These water weeds provide shelter for such creatures as water snails, worms, freshwater shrimps and leeches. There are also many larvae of insects such as stoneflies, mayflies and caddis flies. In deeper water there are such creatures as water-fleas (daphnia) and the fishes that feed on them.

RIVER REACHES

Rivers can be classified according to how fast the water flows through them. The water is faster and more *turbulent* (churned up) in mountainous regions, and slower and more gentle in the flat plains. The speed of the water, plus its depth and temperature, affect the type of fish found in a particular reach. For example, trout like fast, cold mountain streams, whereas bream prefer deeper and warmer slow-running rivers.

From its source to its mouth, a river can be divided into four zones, each one named after the fish most commonly found there. They are the trout, minnow, chub and bream regions.

Mayfly

Stonefly and nymph

Miller's thumb

Brown trout

Grayling

Dipper

Minnow

Kingfisher

Monkey flower

Yellow iris

Purple loosestrife

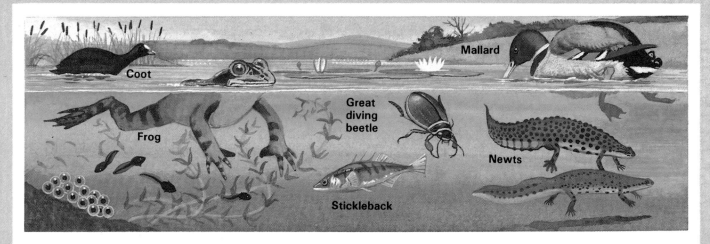

POND LIFE

However quiet a pond may look on the surface, it is a busy place under water. Frogs lay their eggs there, and the eggs hatch into wriggling, active tadpoles. The frogs' relatives, the newts, also lay their eggs in water, and the warty newts tend to stay there all the time.

The many fishes include sticklebacks. At breeding time the male stickleback builds a nest of bits of plant, in which the female lays her eggs.

Many nymphs, the young of certain insects, live in water, and so do some adults, though they have to come to the surface to breathe.

The great diving beetle, over 1½ inches long, attacks almost any living thing in the pond, including small fishes.

Water birds include ducks, swans and coots, which feed on fish and insects. The commonest duck is the mallard, which nests on shore.

Below: A panorama of the rich and varied life to be found in and close to a river, from its source in the mountains to the time it flows into the sea. The stonefly and the mayfly are two insects well known to fishermen, because they are popular food for the brown trout, which gives its name to this stretch of the river. The insects' larvae are eaten by such fish as the miller's thumb, also called the bullhead. In the same region is the dipper, a bird that stands on the stream bed watching for food, mostly insects.

In the next stretch the minnow and grayling are common fishes. The minnow is a popular food for the brightly-colored kingfisher.

Roach are found when the stream is flowing at a moderate pace. They also feed on insect larvae, such as the young of dragonflies, and on various plants. Moorhens nest on the banks. Nearer the sea, perch are abundant, and in the river mouth such sea fishes as flounder and mullet live. Herons fish in the shallows.

Some of the wild flowers to be found in or near streams are shown along the bottom of the picture. The sea aster is a coastal plant.

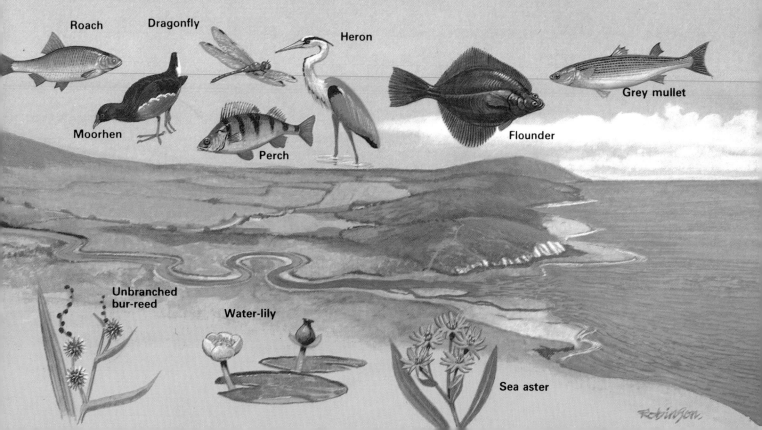

Gull

Hawk

Goose

Pigeon

Tern

Cormorant

Buzzard

Birds of the Air

Birds are animals with wings and feathers. Most of them can fly, and to make this possible their bones are very light and very strong. There are about 9,000 different species. The most familiar are the perching birds, which have claws that grasp twigs and branches. They include all the garden songbirds. Birds with webbed feet for swimming spend their lives in or near water. Birds of prey hunt other birds and small mammals. Birds such as the kiwi cannot fly.

Above: Birds in flight can often be identified by their outlines, seen against the sky. Some typical outlines are shown here. Small animals learn to recognise birds of prey and quickly seek shelter from their sharp talons.

Below: Birds' feet are shaped to suit the kind of life they lead – climbing, perching, swimming or running.

Below: The talons of a golden eagle are shaped for seizing prey such as this young rabbit, which is just able to reach the safety of its hole.

Swimming (Mallard)

Running (Partridge)

Perching (Greenfinch)

Climbing (Woodpecker)

BEAKS

Toucan

Flesh-tearing beak
(Griffon vulture)

Seed-cracking
beak (Chaffinch)

Chisel-like beak
(Woodpecker)

Mud-probing
beak (Curlew)

Fish-scooping
bill (Pelican)

Crow

Pheasant

Swift

Hummingbird
drinking nectar

Above: Beaks are shaped to deal with the different kinds of food. The short, stout beak of the chaffinch, for example, is ideal for eating seeds. And the long beak of a hummingbird is adapted to probing deep into flowers for nectar. But the value of its huge, gaily-coloured beak to the fruit-eating toucan is unknown.

Birds range in size from the ostrich, which is up to 8 feet tall and weighs 340 lbs, to the bee humming-bird, only 2 ins long including the tail, and weighing less than 1/10 ounce.

As a rule, male birds are more brightly colored than the females, and they use their smart feathers to help them when courting. One reason for the duller colors of females is that it helps them to be less conspicuous when sitting on the nest hatching their eggs, and so less likely to fall victim to predators.

Although all birds have some kind of voice, only about a third of them are real singers. Ornithologists – people who study birds – are not really sure why birds sing: some appear to sing in order to warn off rivals, others sing to attract mates. But some do seem to sing just for pleasure.

Birds have very varied diets. Some feed mostly on seeds, and have strong beaks to break open the seed cases. The finches are examples of seed-eaters. Birds such as thrushes feed on insects and worms, and many birds have a mixed diet of insects and seeds.

The seabirds, such as gulls, catch fish, using their long bills to seize them. Hawks and other birds of prey feed on small animals. Birds such as vultures eat carrion, the dead bodies of animals.

Birds have many ways of flying. The broad wings of eagles and hawks enable them to soar and hover in the sky, looking for prey. The long narrow wings of swallows give them great speed, which they need because they catch insects in the air. The even longer wings of the albatross enable it to stay airborne at sea for days at a time.

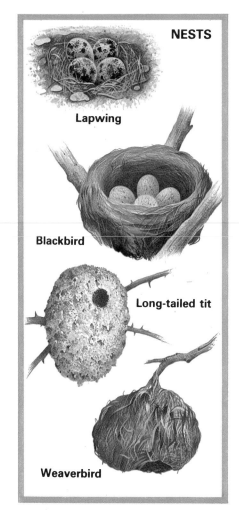

NESTS

Lapwing

Blackbird

Long-tailed tit

Weaverbird

Seal

Musk ox

Polar bear

Skunk

Fox

EUROPE

Badger

NORTH AMERICA

Bald eagle

Puma

Swallow

Giraffe

Chimpanzee

World Wildlife

About 200 million years ago, when dinosaurs roamed the Earth, the continents were joined together in a vast supercontinent called Pangaea. But slowly the continents drifted apart and animals living on one land mass became separated from those living on another. Each group of animals continued to change – to *evolve* – but, isolated from each other, they evolved in different ways. This is why, today, certain animals are found only on certain continents; why, for example, kangaroos are found only in Australia and llamas only in South America. The map shows animals typical of each area.

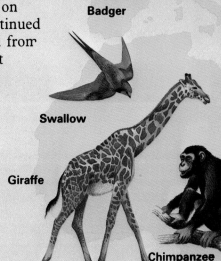

Anaconda

SOUTH AMERICA

Scarlet macaw

Sloth

Llama

Armadillo

Springbok

NORTH AMERICA

Only a narrow stretch of water separates North America from Asia. Often in the past the two land masses have been joined by a land bridge, and animals have been able to pass from one to the other. For this reason, many of the animals found in North America are closely related to those found in Asia and Europe.

SOUTH AMERICA

South America has many animals found nowhere else in the world. Some are quite strange in both appearance and behavior, such as the sloth, spending its days hanging upside-down in the trees, or the toothless anteater, rummaging through ant hills with its long nose. There is also a wealth of beautiful birds such as the scarlet macaw in the tropical rain forests.

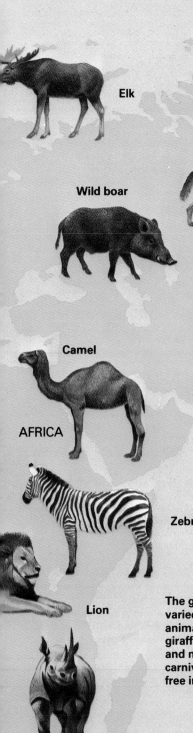

Elk

Wild boar

Wolf

Crane

Giant panda

ASIA

Indian elephant

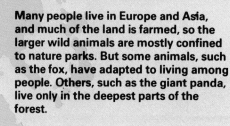

EUROPE AND ASIA

Many people live in Europe and Asia, and much of the land is farmed, so the larger wild animals are mostly confined to nature parks. But some animals, such as the fox, have adapted to living among people. Others, such as the giant panda, live only in the deepest parts of the forest.

Camel

AFRICA

Tiger

Zebra

Lion

AFRICA

The grasslands of Africa have the most varied collection of large grazing animals in the world — including the giraffe, elephant, rhinoceros, antelopes and many others. These animals and the carnivores which prey on them roam free in vast national parks.

Bird of paradise

Kangaroo

Koala

Rhinoceros

AUSTRALASIA

Australia was the first continent to break away from Pangaea. It did so at a time when most of the world's mammals reared their young in pouches. These animals, called marsupials, flourished in Australia, but soon became extinct in other parts of the world. The koala and kangaroo are both marsupials, and are found only in Australia. The tuatara, a reptile found in New Zealand, is the nearest living relative of the great dinosaurs.

Emu

Tuatara

AUSTRALIA

Kiwi

NEW ZEALAND

35

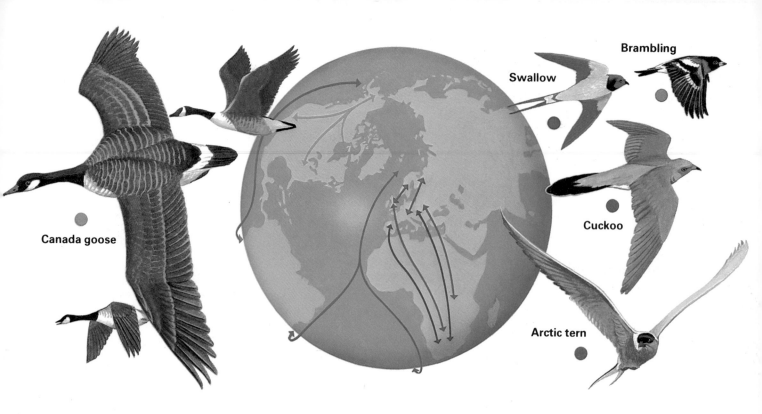

Swallow

Brambling

Canada goose

Cuckoo

Arctic tern

Animal Journeys

In search of food, or a place to breed and rear their young, many animals make long journeys each year. This annual traveling is called *migration*.

Birds are the best known migrants. Many spend the summer months in cooler lands and fly to warmer places for the winter. Swallows, for instance, arrive in Europe in late spring. They build their nests, rear their young, and feast upon insects. Then, as the fall days grow shorter, they leave in great flocks. Guided only by instinct they fly south to Africa.

Other animals that migrate include many fishes, whales and seals, some insects, especially butterflies, and the large grazing animals such as deer and antelope.

Above: Some of the routes taken by migrating birds. The Arctic tern flies from the Arctic to the Antarctic and back in search of perpetual summer.

Below left: Seals migrate to their breeding grounds in spring, then return to warmer seas in winter.
Below centre: Salmon spend most of their lives at sea, but return to the rivers where they were born to breed their own young.
Below right: Sea turtles come to land in the same places every year to lay their eggs.

Navigation

Sailors and airmen use a great variety of aids to navigate across the world – compasses, maps, charts, radar, and chronometers for keeping accurate time. But birds have traveled for millions of years without any of these things to guide them.

After experimenting with starlings and homing pigeons, scientists came to the conclusion that they and many other birds navigate by means of the Sun and the stars. Other experiments suggest that birds can detect the magnetic field of the Earth, just as a compass needle does.

Right: The Monarch butterfly of North America makes one of the longest migrations undertaken by any insect. In summer these butterflies are found in North America as far north as the shores of Hudson Bay. Their young migrate south to Florida and Mexico, where they hibernate on trees. In spring they fly back to the north.

Below: The Sargasso Sea is a region of the western Atlantic Ocean that is full of densely floating seaweed. In these quiet waters baby eels hatch from their eggs. At this stage they look like tiny willow leaves. They drift slowly east across the Atlantic, growing until they turn into elvers, the next stage of development. They travel up rivers and turn into adult eels. After several years they return to the Sargasso to lay their eggs and die.

Below: The musk ox is a strange animal, midway between a sheep and an ox. Musk oxen roam in herds, feeding on grass in the river valleys of north-east Canada and Greenland in the summer, and migrating to higher ground in winter. There, the wind blows much of the snow away so they can get at the vegetation beneath. The animals form a tight circle when wolves threaten them.

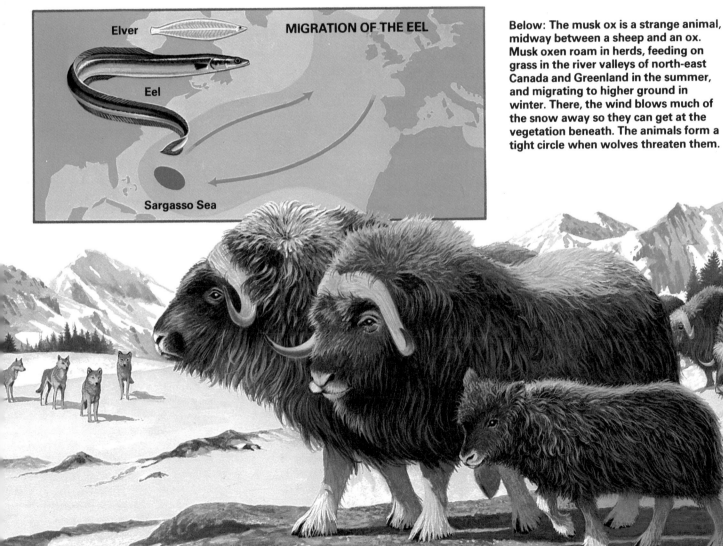

Elver

MIGRATION OF THE EEL

Eel

Sargasso Sea

Animal Homes

Animals such as antelopes, bison and elephants which roam the wide plains do not have a settled home. Birds and many insects construct temporary homes in which to lay their eggs and rear their young. Some animals build permanent homes for themselves, often with great skill. This skill is not something they learn, but is born in them, and is part of that mysterious quality known as instinct.

Only a few mammals build homes, and they are mostly the smaller creatures, which construct burrows underground. Often these underground homes are for more than one family. For example, marmots, living mostly in mountain districts, form colonies of 10 to 15 animals. Prairie dogs, found in North America, have similar-sized colonies, but link them together to form large 'towns'. Badgers and foxes are among the larger mammals that tunnel into the ground to make their homes.

The Nest Builders
Some other small mammals, such as mice and squirrels, build nests. These nests are not unlike the nests of birds, and are constructed by weaving together twigs, stalks and pieces of leaves.

Right: The tiny harvest mouse builds its nest among the stalks of reeds, long grass, or growing cereal crops. Like other rodents, its front paws are almost like hands, which greatly helps it in its work. A harvest mouse can complete its nest in less than 10 hours.

The best-known home builders are birds. Most of them build afresh every year, but some, such as the white stork of Europe, merely clean up and repair the same nests year after year.

Nest-building techniques vary a great deal. Birds whose young are born with feathers and can leave the nest almost at once make very simple nests. Swans and ducks do this. Most chicks, however, are helpless to begin with and need a warm, secure place to grow up in.

Birds use a great variety of materials, often whatever is handy. A sparrow in Switzerland, home of the watch industry, even built a nest entirely of watch springs! Tailorbirds stitch the large leaves of trees or shrubs together to form a bag, which they line with soft materials. Storks use large twigs, often reinforced with rags, straw and mud. Mud is the

Harvest mice are among the smallest mice in the world: a single specimen weighs $\frac{3}{10}$ ounce; its length is 8 inches. Half of this is the tail, used to help in climbing.

main material used by swallows, swifts and martins. Woodpeckers, with their chisel-like beaks, make holes in tree-trunks.

A few fishes, such as salmon and sticklebacks, build nests to lay their eggs in, but the jawfishes build actual homes: deep wells lined with pebbles, where they lie in wait for their prey.

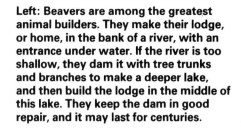

Left: Beavers are among the greatest animal builders. They make their lodge, or home, in the bank of a river, with an entrance under water. If the river is too shallow, they dam it with tree trunks and branches to make a deeper lake, and then build the lodge in the middle of this lake. They keep the dam in good repair, and it may last for centuries.

Below: Termites are the most skilled insect builders. Some species build mounds as much as 23 feet high, and they equip them with ventilating shafts. They also bore wells to get water.

1

2

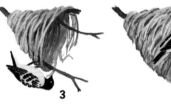

3

4

Left: Badgers generally make their home, called a set, in or on the edge of a wood. A well established badger set can be up to 16 feet deep, and cover an area 33 yards across. A large set of this kind has many rooms and passages, with several entrances, and is usually home for more than one family. Badgers are very clean animals; from time to time they take their bedding out and air it, and they dig their latrines at a little distance from the set. Sometimes foxes move into part of a badger set, but the badgers then wall off the foxes' home to keep out the smell.

Above: There are many species of weaverbirds, but the work of the village weaver of East Africa is a typical example:
1 The male bird selects a forked twig of a tree and starts to twist strips of leaf round it. He uses blades of grass or strips torn off palm leaves.
2 Gradually the nest starts to take shape.
3 The bird knots strands on to the twig, or on to other strands, and weaves them in and out as if using a loom.
4 The finished nest has a long flight tube as an entrance.

Friends and Foes

Above: The speedy cheetah makes a dash to catch an antelope. But if the antelope can keep running the cheetah soon tires and gives up the chase.

Above: The pangolin, or scaly anteater, rolls itself into a ball when danger threatens.

Below: The Australian frilled lizard tries to frighten away its attackers by hissing and spreading out a fold of skin.

Animals in the wild have few friends, and many enemies. On land, the grazing animals, such as deer, antelopes, elephants and bison form large herds. A herd itself is a protection against danger, but often the stronger animals deliberately guard the weaker; for example, when musk oxen form their protective circle they place the younger animals in the centre.

In the sea, fish often stay together in huge shoals, and so do many species of whales. Whales and dolphins have been seen supporting and escorting an injured companion.

Animal Partners
Some of the most remarkable 'friendships' are those between animals of different species. They live together for mutual support, a state known as *symbiosis*. The hermit crab lives in a discarded shell, and has a sea anemone on the outside of the shell. The stinging cells of the sea anemone

Kadydid

Stick insect

Treble bar moth

Leaf insect

Crab spider

protect the crab, and the anemone benefits from food particles discarded by the crab. When the crab grows and moves to a bigger shell, it takes its sea anemone with it.

Little fishes known as wrasses living in the Indian and Pacific oceans act as cleaners for bigger fish. They eat parasites, such as fish-lice, on the bodies of the larger fish, which queue up to be cleaned.

When Danger Threatens

Danger in the wild comes from the *carnivores*, the flesh-eaters, who prey on the *herbivores*, the plant-eaters. The term 'carnivore' includes not only such large animals as tigers and hyenas, but also many birds which prey on small creatures such as insects.

Some animals, such as the springbok, rely on their speed to escape from danger. The hedgehog curls up, presenting a predator with an unappetising ball of prickles. Many animals have *protective coloration*: their coloring matches that of their background. For example, a white Arctic hare is hard to see against snow. Small creatures often look like something else: there are moths which resemble bird droppings, insects which look like leaves or twigs, and plaice which match the sea bed on which they lie. Many creatures, such as wasps, are harmful to eat, and have *warning coloration*, generally red or yellow and black. Other animals mimic this coloration, even though they are not unpleasant to eat; for example, hoverflies look very like wasps.

Above: Some examples of insect camouflage on a tree trunk. At the top a katydid nestles among leaves of a similar color. The stick insect poses to look just like a twig on the side of the tree, while the treble bar moth has coloring like the trunk itself. The leaf-insect 'hides' by sitting openly on a leaf. Even bright colors can be a camouflage, as can be seen in the yellow crab spider crouched on a buttercup awaiting its prey.

Right: Oxpeckers are African starlings which spend their lives living on large animals, such as the Cape buffalo shown here. They feed on ticks and other parasites which they pull out of the animals' skin. They warn their hosts when danger is about by uttering loud cries and flying about in the air. The large animals take no notice of their companions except when they give the alarm. The birds make their nests in holes in trees, or in rocks.

41

The World of Plants

Without plants there would be no other life on Earth. For only plants can make their own food using simple materials – carbon dioxide gas from the air and water and mineral salts from the ground. Animals cannot make their own food: they feed either upon plants or upon each other. Plants also provide shade and shelter: birds, insects and mammals make their homes in trees.

There are about 500,000 species of plants, and they are classified in a similar way to animals. Many species of plants share the same common names.

Right: The ripened seeds of flowering plants need to be widely scattered if the new plants are to spread and survive. Birds eat many of the juicy fruits, and the hard seeds pass through them and are scattered that way. Pods of peas and beans burst when they are ripe, hurling their seeds a considerable distance. Very light seeds such as those of dandelions and grasses are carried by the wind, and so are the heavier winged seeds of the sycamore.

The Plant Kingdom

There are several groups of simple plants: algae, which include seaweeds and the scum on ponds; fungi, such as toadstools; liverworts, and mosses. Then come the fern-type plants: ferns, clubmosses, and horsetails.

The next group of plants is called the *gymnosperms*, which means 'naked seeds'. They have their egg cells and pollen in cones, and include cycads, ginkgoes, and the familiar conifers. Finally come the flowering plants, known as the *angiosperms*, which means 'seeds in a case'.

All plants except the simplest work in the same way. A typical plant has a system of roots, which anchor it in the soil and also absorb water and minerals from the soil. The stem carries the water from the roots to the leaves. It also supports the leaves and raises them up to catch the light.

Trees, bushes and shrubs have woody stems. The wood in the middle of a tree trunk is very hard and no longer carries water, but it provides a strong support for the tree. The trunk grows a little thicker every year and you can tell the age of a tree stump by counting the number of growth rings across its trunk.

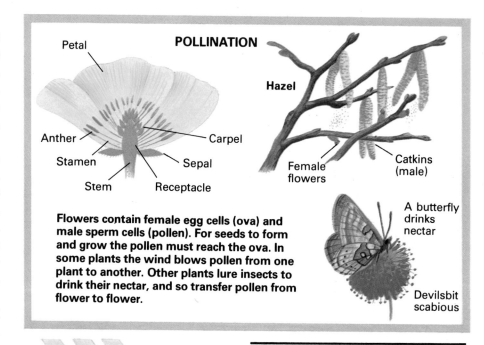

POLLINATION

Petal

Anther

Stamen

Stem

Carpel

Sepal

Receptacle

Hazel

Female flowers

Catkins (male)

A butterfly drinks nectar

Devilsbit scabious

Flowers contain female egg cells (ova) and male sperm cells (pollen). For seeds to form and grow the pollen must reach the ova. In some plants the wind blows pollen from one plant to another. Other plants lure insects to drink their nectar, and so transfer pollen from flower to flower.

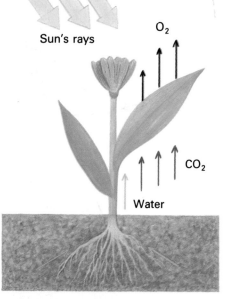

Sun's rays

O_2

CO_2

Water

PHOTOSYNTHESIS

The process by which plants make their food is *photosynthesis,* which means 'building with light'. Most of the work is done by the leaves. They contain a green coloring substance called chlorophyll, which absorbs some of the light falling on the leaves and uses it as a source of energy for chemical changes. The leaves absorb carbon dioxide (CO_2) from the air, and water from the roots. They turn this CO_2 and water into sugar, which in turn can be turned into other substances to build up the plant's structure. The plant cannot use all the oxygen in carbon dioxide, and gives it off as oxygen gas (O_2). All animals need oxygen to live, and plants keep up the supply.

Thrush eating
hawthorn berry

Parachute-like
seed of dandelion

Wind blowing
grass seeds

GERMINATION

1   2   3   4

When a seed falls on soil and the
weather is warm enough – as in
spring – it begins to germinate, that
is, to grow. The seed absorbs water
and swells, the case bursts open,
and a root appears, followed by the
first shoot.
Germination can be studied by
putting a bean in a jar lined with

blotting paper and keeping the
paper moist (1). Soon the young
root bursts from the seed (2) and
always grows downwards (3).
Finally the shoot springs up (4) and
the first leaves are formed. Once
this happens the plant can begin to
make its own food and grow
rapidly.

Goldfinch eating
plantain seeds

Dandelion
'clock'
shedding
seeds

Thistle
seedling

Thistles

Winged seeds
of sycamore

Poppy seeds
falling from
a seed pod

Dormouse nibbling
hawthorn berry

Ant carrying
poppy seed

Nature Trails

The best way to find out about animals and plants is to take a walk in the country, or even take a look in a town park.

Many national parks and country parks have nature trails marked out to lead naturalists to the places where they can see the most interesting plants and animals. They often provide identification plates similar to those opposite, to help people to put a name to what they see.

Most naturalists following nature trails find that it is a good plan to take a notebook and pencil, to make a record of anything they see, and even a sketch to help identification later. Binoculars are a great help for studying birds, and a pocket magnifying glass is essential to find out the details of plants which may look alike to the casual eye.

There is another form of nature trail, too – that left by the feet of animals as they go about their daily lives. Such footprints show up best in snow, but they can also be detected in soft ground, and even in dewy grass. There are other marks, too, that betray the presence of animals, such as the claw marks which badgers leave on the trees and logs they use as scratching posts, or holes in a bank which are home to some small creatures.

The best time to see and identify tracks left by animals is when snow is on the ground. Remember animals leave slightly different marks according to the way they are moving, and this shows up clearly in snow.

Fox, trotting

Badger, bounding

Roe deer

Rabbit

Shrew

Oak

Birch

Lombardy
poplar

Scots pine

Larch

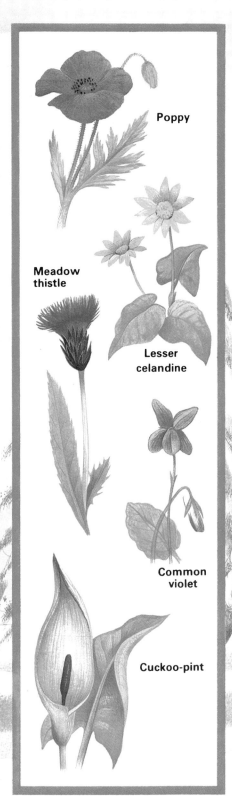

Poppy

Meadow
thistle

Lesser
celandine

Common
violet

Cuckoo-pint

Tawny
owl

Swallow

Redstart

Lapwing

Pochard

Mouse,
bounding

Rabbit,
hopping slowly

Stoat, bounding

Squirrel, jumping

Your Body

If you could look inside your body, you would see a magnificent machine at work – more magnificent than any machine a person could build. As you are looking at this book, reading the words and understanding them, your body is breathing, hearing, moving, feeling, digesting your last meal, making you hungry for the next, and performing hundreds more tasks without you even noticing. The different parts of the body do different jobs and each part depends on the others.

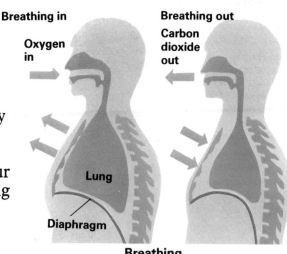

Breathing in — Oxygen in

Breathing out — Carbon dioxide out

Lung

Diaphragm

Breathing

We all need the gas oxygen to stay alive and we give our bodies a steady supply by breathing. When we breathe in our ribs move upwards, expanding the chest, and a flat muscle beneath the lungs moves downwards. This sucks air into our lungs, which fill up like two big balloons. Oxygen then passes through the thin walls of the lungs into the blood, and a waste gas, carbon dioxide, passes out of the blood to be exhaled when we breathe out.

Bones and Bending

Your body gets its shape from its frame of bones – your skeleton. Without your skeleton you would be just a blob. The bones hold you up and enable you to move. There are lots of bones of different sizes and they meet at joints. Your elbow is a joint, so are your shoulders and your hips and your knees. Your elbow works like a hinge moving backwards and forwards. Your shoulder joint lets your arm move right round like a ball in a socket. Which way do your hips and knees work?

Bones do not move by themselves. They are moved by muscles which are attached to them. Muscles work in pairs, one working, one resting.

Digesting our Food

A machine needs fuel to make its parts work. Our fuel is our food. When we swallow food it goes down a pipe to the stomach and mixes with chemicals which break it down into a liquid. This goes into the intestines, a coiled tube which churns up the liquid food until it is pure enough to go into our blood.

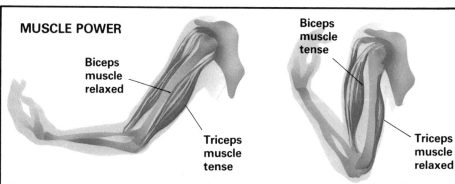

MUSCLE POWER

Biceps muscle relaxed

Triceps muscle tense

Biceps muscle tense

Triceps muscle relaxed

Stretch out your arm and feel the muscle above your elbow. Then bend your arm and feel how much shorter and harder the muscle is. It is pulling hard to keep your arm up. When you let your arm go the muscle will relax again and lie flat. The muscle at the back of your arm will then be tense.

Skin Deep

On the outside of your body is your skin. It is not just a layer that keeps everything else inside, like a paper bag, it is alive and working, keeping you warm and dry and safe from harm. The tiny hairs in your skin keep you warm but if you get too hot your skin sweats. Water oozes from its surface and cools you down.

Hair

Sweat gland

Oil gland

Hair follicle

Fat

Muscle

Nerve

Blood vessels

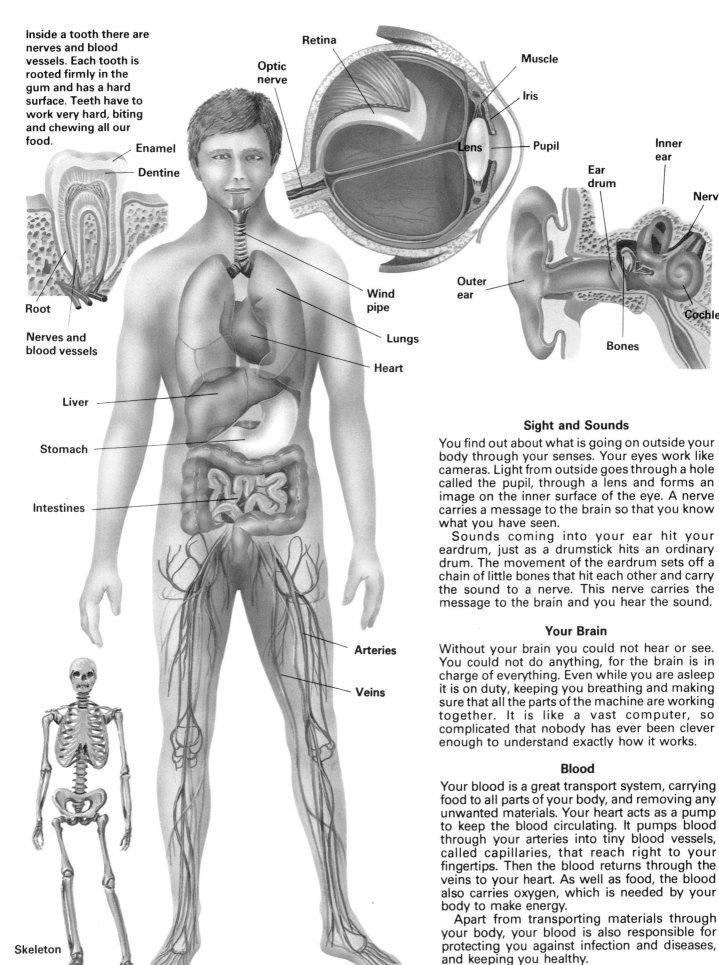

Inside a tooth there are nerves and blood vessels. Each tooth is rooted firmly in the gum and has a hard surface. Teeth have to work very hard, biting and chewing all our food.

Retina

Optic nerve

Muscle

Iris

Enamel

Dentine

Lens

Pupil

Inner ear

Ear drum

Nerve

Root

Nerves and blood vessels

Outer ear

Bones

Cochlea

Wind pipe

Lungs

Heart

Liver

Stomach

Intestines

Arteries

Veins

Skeleton

Sight and Sounds

You find out about what is going on outside your body through your senses. Your eyes work like cameras. Light from outside goes through a hole called the pupil, through a lens and forms an image on the inner surface of the eye. A nerve carries a message to the brain so that you know what you have seen.

Sounds coming into your ear hit your eardrum, just as a drumstick hits an ordinary drum. The movement of the eardrum sets off a chain of little bones that hit each other and carry the sound to a nerve. This nerve carries the message to the brain and you hear the sound.

Your Brain

Without your brain you could not hear or see. You could not do anything, for the brain is in charge of everything. Even while you are asleep it is on duty, keeping you breathing and making sure that all the parts of the machine are working together. It is like a vast computer, so complicated that nobody has ever been clever enough to understand exactly how it works.

Blood

Your blood is a great transport system, carrying food to all parts of your body, and removing any unwanted materials. Your heart acts as a pump to keep the blood circulating. It pumps blood through your arteries into tiny blood vessels, called capillaries, that reach right to your fingertips. Then the blood returns through the veins to your heart. As well as food, the blood also carries oxygen, which is needed by your body to make energy.

Apart from transporting materials through your body, your blood is also responsible for protecting you against infection and diseases, and keeping you healthy.

47

Records in Nature

HIGHEST MOUNTAINS (feet)

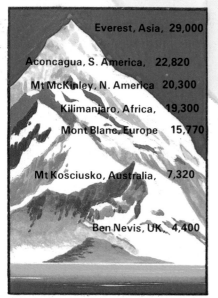

Everest, Asia, 29,000

Aconcagua, S. America, 22,820

Mt McKinley, N. America 20,300

Kilimanjaro, Africa, 19,300

Mont Blanc, Europe 15,770

Mt Kosciusko, Australia, 7,320

Ben Nevis, UK, 4,400

Above: During the Earth's long history, many mountain ranges have been created by movements in the rocks, and then gradually worn away by water, wind and ice. The highest peaks today are in the youngest mountain ranges – the Himalayas, Andes, Rockies and Alps. There may well have been higher mountain peaks millions of years ago.

There is a great range in the size of living things. At one end of the scale there are viruses – organisms on the very borders of life – which are too small to be seen without the aid of powerful electron microscopes. At the other extreme there is the blue whale which can weigh over 115 tons, and the Californian redwood tree which grows as high as a 35-storey building.

The life-span of living things also varies greatly. Small insects, such as the mayfly, have an adult life-span which can be measured in days or even hours, while the tortoise may live for 150 years or more. Some plants, especially trees, live far longer. There are giant sequoia trees in California which began life almost 4,000 years ago, and bristlecone pines which are as old as the pyramids.

LONGEST RIVERS (approx. miles)

Nile, Africa, 4,150

Mississippi-Missouri, N. America, 3,900

Amazon, S. America, 3,880

Yangtze, Asia, 3,200

Congo, Africa, 2,850

Amur, Asia, 2,850

Lena, Asia, 2,750

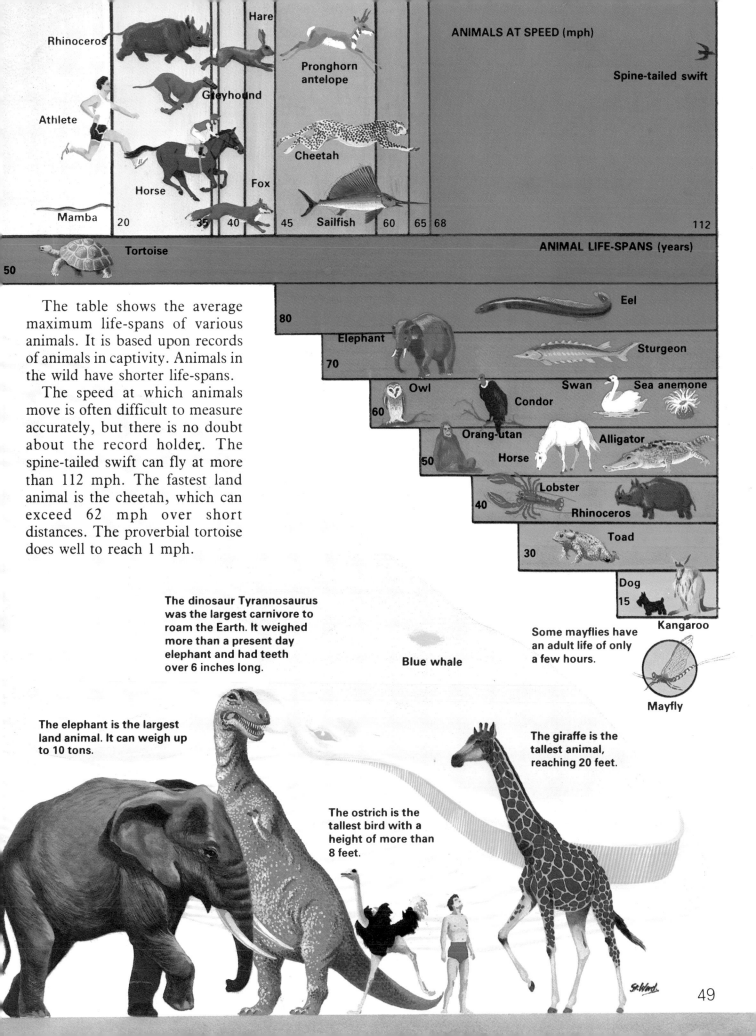

ANIMALS AT SPEED (mph)

Rhinoceros
Hare
Pronghorn antelope
Spine-tailed swift
Greyhound
Athlete
Cheetah
Horse
Fox
Mamba
Sailfish
20 — 35 — 40 — 45 — 60 — 65 — 68 — 112

ANIMAL LIFE-SPANS (years)

Tortoise
50

Eel
80

Elephant
70

Sturgeon

Owl
60
Condor
Swan
Sea anemone

Orang-utan
50
Horse
Alligator

Lobster
40
Rhinoceros

Toad
30

Dog
15
Kangaroo

The table shows the average maximum life-spans of various animals. It is based upon records of animals in captivity. Animals in the wild have shorter life-spans.

The speed at which animals move is often difficult to measure accurately, but there is no doubt about the record holder. The spine-tailed swift can fly at more than 112 mph. The fastest land animal is the cheetah, which can exceed 62 mph over short distances. The proverbial tortoise does well to reach 1 mph.

The dinosaur Tyrannosaurus was the largest carnivore to roam the Earth. It weighed more than a present day elephant and had teeth over 6 inches long.

Blue whale

Some mayflies have an adult life of only a few hours.

Mayfly

The elephant is the largest land animal. It can weigh up to 10 tons.

The ostrich is the tallest bird with a height of more than 8 feet.

The giraffe is the tallest animal, reaching 20 feet.

49

Above: A horse painted on the wall of Le Portel Cave, in France, 20,000 years ago.
Right: Some of the simple stone tools made by Stone Age men. They include spears, an axe, a hammer, a scraper, and a needle made of bone.

The First People

Man and the apes are descended from a common ancestor that lived many millions of years ago. Man-like creatures, hominids, have been roaming the Earth for more than two million years. The oldest remains of Man have been found in Africa.

Modern Man, often called Cro-Magnon Man, from a cave in France where his skeletons were first discovered, came into Europe from the East about 40,000 years ago. Nobody knows for certain when these people first lived, or where. For about a hundred thousand years before this, another group of early people lived in Europe. They were the Neanderthal Men, named after a valley in Germany where they were first identified. Neanderthal Man was probably the first cave-dweller. He was a heavier, clumsier person than modern Man, but he had a large brain, he made tools and hunted, and he buried his dead with elaborate ceremonies.

All these early people are often called Stone Age people, because they made nearly all their tools and implements from hard stones, such as flints. A flint knife can be sharp enough to cut up raw meat easily. Using flint scrapers, Stone Age Man made other tools from wood, bone, and the antlers of deer.

Early Man lived in caves. He hunted animals such as deer for food, and he knew how to make fire. He often had to fend off animals such as the great cave bear.

Neanderthal Man

Modern Man

Chimpanzee

51

The Ancient World

Great Wall of China

Ziggurat at Ur

Civilization is a word which means 'living in a city'. The first cities grew up in the Fertile Crescent, an area which ran northwards from the Persian Gulf, through present-day Iraq and round to Egypt.

The earliest civilizations were those of Sumer, Babylonia and Assyria, all in Iraq. The ruins of many of these cities have been found, such as those of Ur, birthplace of Abraham. These cities had *ziggurats*, great towering temples. The ancient Egyptians carried the ziggurat idea further by building pyramids, huge stone structures which served as tombs.

A debate among a group of Greek philosophers

Bull-leaping at Knossos, in Crete

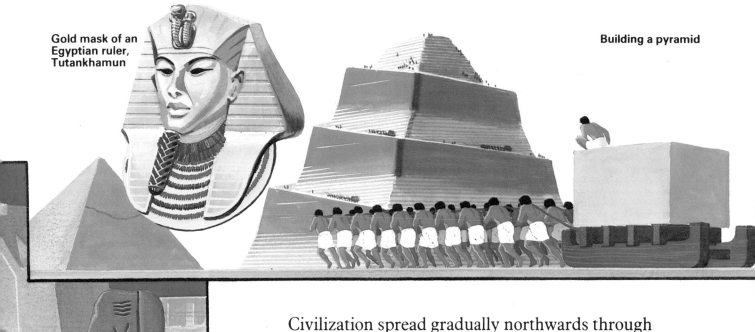

Gold mask of an Egyptian ruler, Tutankhamun

Building a pyramid

Ancient writing

A Grecian urn

The Grecian statue of Venus

Civilization spread gradually northwards through Palestine and the Bible lands. The first civilization in Europe was that of the Minoans, who lived on the island of Crete in the Mediterranean. They are famous for the Minotaur, a mythical monster, and for the dangerous sport of bull-leaping – jumping over a bull by holding on to its horns. The Cretan civilization was closely connected with that of mainland Greece. The Greeks were very clever people. They included some of the greatest architects and sculptors the world has ever known, and also some of the finest thinkers. *Philosophy*, the science of thought, and *democracy*, government by the people, were both evolved by the Greeks.

The Romans, originating at Rome in Italy, were mighty soldiers and conquerors. They built up an empire covering a large part of Europe and North Africa. They were fond of sports such as chariot races, and fights between men known as gladiators. The Chinese civilization is also very old. The Chinese built their Great Wall to keep out invaders at about the time the Romans were creating their empire.

Roman chariot race

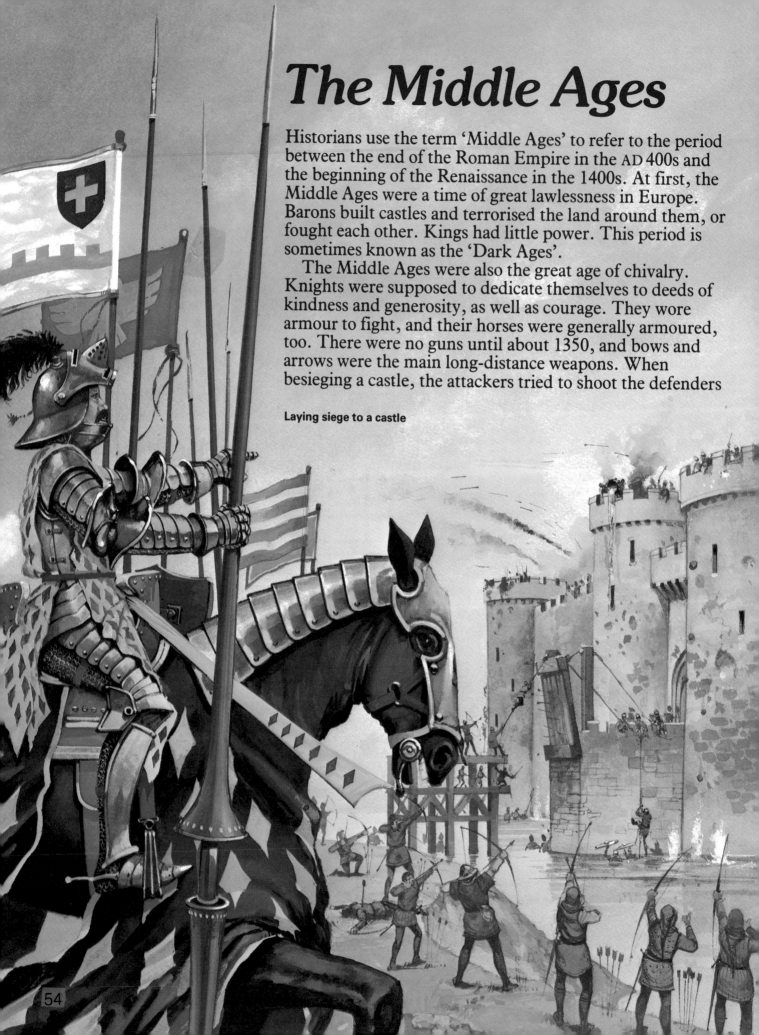

The Middle Ages

Historians use the term 'Middle Ages' to refer to the period between the end of the Roman Empire in the AD 400s and the beginning of the Renaissance in the 1400s. At first, the Middle Ages were a time of great lawlessness in Europe. Barons built castles and terrorised the land around them, or fought each other. Kings had little power. This period is sometimes known as the 'Dark Ages'.

The Middle Ages were also the great age of chivalry. Knights were supposed to dedicate themselves to deeds of kindness and generosity, as well as courage. They wore armour to fight, and their horses were generally armoured, too. There were no guns until about 1350, and bows and arrows were the main long-distance weapons. When besieging a castle, the attackers tried to shoot the defenders

Laying siege to a castle

The Black Death, an epidemic of bubonic plague, swept Europe in the 1300s, killing one person in four.

Below: When the lord of the manor was away at the wars he left his estates in the charge of a reeve, or bailiff, who dealt with the peasants and other workers.

Bottom: The 'Mona Lisa' is a painting by Leonardo da Vinci, one of the greatest artists of the Renaissance. It is now in Paris.

on the walls, and to throw up ropes with grappling irons so that they could climb the walls. The defenders responded by dropping rocks and boiling oil on their assailants.

In many countries of Europe, people lived under the feudal system, a term which comes from the word 'feu' meaning fee or services. The system worked as follows: the king held all the land, and gave some of it to his barons in return for military service in time of war. The barons let some of their land to knights or lesser nobles on the same terms, and so on down the line to ordinary peasants – small farmers. There were also serfs, who had no land and were virtually slaves. In later times, the military service gave way to a payment of money, which the king could use to hire soldiers when he needed them. The chief landowner of an area was called the Lord of the Manor.

The New Age of Learning

Very few people could read or write outside the Church. Learning was kept alive by the monks and priests, who also made copies of all books, because there was no printing in those days.

By the end of the Middle Ages things were changing rapidly. Scholars in Italy became interested in the work and learning of classical Greece and Rome, and so began the Renaissance – a word which means 'rebirth' and describes the renewal of interest in learning. It was helped by the invention of printing in the 1440s, which enabled books to be more widely available. New ideas in art and architecture were developed, too.

Explorers

We owe our knowledge of the world today to the courage and endurance of the men who set out to explore the unknown. Some of the earliest explorers were the boldest because they had the greatest fears, such as Bartholomeu Dias, whose crew thought they would sail over the edge of a flat Earth. Courage and endurance are still needed, as shown by the adventures of John Blashford-Snell and a British-American party who fought their way through the swamp and jungle of the Darien Gap in Central America.

NOTABLE DATES IN EXPLORATION

300 BC Pythias of Massilia was the first Greek to explore beyond the Mediterranean. He reached England.

AD 629–643 The Chinese philosopher Hsüan-tsang explored central Asia and India.

1000 Viking Leif Ericsson visited the shores of North America.

1271–1295 Venetian merchant Marco Polo travelled to China, and from there explored Burma and India.

1325–1349 Moroccan lawyer Ibn Battuta explored East Africa, the Middle East, India, Sri Lanka and China.

1487–1488 Portuguese navigator Bartholomeu Dias became the first European to sail round the Cape of Good Hope.

1492 Italian navigator Christopher Columbus discovered the West Indies.

1498 Portuguese navigator Vasco da Gama made the first sea voyage from Europe to India.

1499 Italian merchant Amerigo Vespucci discovered the mainland of America, now named after him.

1519–1521 Hernán Cortés, a Spanish adventurer, explored and conquered Mexico.

1519–1522 An expedition led by Ferdinand Magellan, a Portuguese navigator, made the first round-the-world voyage; Magellan died on the voyage, which was completed by Juan Sebastián del Cano.

1531 Francisco Pizarro, a Spanish adventurer, explored Peru.

1541 Hernando de Soto, a Spaniard, discovered the Mississippi River.

1606 Dutch navigator Willem Janz became the first European to sight Australia.

1642 Abel Janszoon Tasman, a Dutch explorer, discovered Tasmania and New Zealand.

1768–1779 In three voyages, English navigator James Cook made the first thorough exploration of the Pacific and Antarctic Oceans.

1804–1806 American soldiers Meriwether Lewis and William Clark explored the area between the Missouri and Columbia rivers.

1828–1845 In three expeditions, colonial administrator Charles Sturt explored eastern Australia.

1849–1873 Scottish missionary David Livingstone explored southern and eastern Africa, discovering the Victoria Falls and several lakes.

1860–1861 Robert O'Hara Burke and William John Wills made the first crossing of Australia from south to north, but died on the journey back.

1858 British soldier John Hanning Speke discovered Lake Victoria.

1876–1877 British-American journalist Henry Morton Stanley explored the River Congo (now the Zaire).

1878–1879 Swedish scientist Nils Nordenskjöld made the first voyage through the North-East Passage.

1903–1906 Norwegian Roald Amundsen made the first voyage through the North-West Passage.

1909 American naval engineer Robert Peary led the first party to reach the North Pole.

1911 Roald Amundsen led the first party to reach the South Pole.

1912 Robert Falcon Scott and three other Britons reached the South Pole 39 days after Amundsen, but died on the return journey.

1958 British geologist Vivian Fuchs led the first crossing of Antarctica.

1968–1969 British surveyor Wally Herbert led the first surface crossing of the Arctic Ocean.

1972 British soldier John Blashford-Snell led the first crossing of the Darien Gap, in Panama and Colombia.

Christopher Columbus

Lewis and Clark

Hernán Cortés

David Livingstone

Marco Polo

- - - - Columbus
- - - - Magellan
- - - - Vasco da Gama
- - - - Captain Cook

The map shows the routes of four of the greatest sea voyages. Pictured, clockwise, are Columbus battling across the Atlantic, Livingstone in unknown Africa, Marco Polo in China, Magellan braving the storms in the strait now named after him, Burke and Wills plodding across Australia, Amundsen at the South Pole, Cortés in Mexico, and Lewis and Clark in America.

Ferdinand Magellan

Robert Burke and William Wills

Roald Amundsen at the South Pole

57

Tomorrow's World

The world we live in is changing faster than ever before. The invention of robots and the microchip is bringing about a revolution in the industrial countries. In years to come people should have a better standard of living, better health, better education, and far more leisure time.

But there are many problems facing mankind in the future. There are many millions of people in the poorer countries who do not have enough to eat. Many cannot read or write and they have little medical care. It will take many years and much effort to make their lives anything like as comfortable as our own.

Below: As the Earth's supplies of metals run out it is possible that other planets and their moons will be mined. The metals will be refined in space and then brought back to Earth.

Bottom: There are many schemes to harness the energy of the waves. One scheme involves large tanks or 'ducks' being rocked up and down by the waves. The motion of the tanks would be used to drive an electricity generator.

In richer countries there are other problems. The consumption of energy and raw materials, for instance, is so great that the Earth is running short of many of its riches. Unless vast new oilfields are found the world will run out of gasoline within thirty years at the present rate of consumption. And the supply of certain metals such as copper and tin will last little longer. That is why scientists are searching for alternative sources of energy, such as harnessing the heat of the Sun and the motion of the waves. For the same reason the recycling of materials will become more important.

58

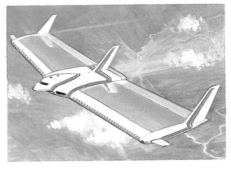

Above: The shape of tomorrow's transport is already on the drawing boards. The main feature of all the designs is that they will use as little energy as possible.

Below: In the future self-supporting colonies will probably be established in space. They may take the form of huge spinning rings. The spin would create artificial gravity for the colonists.

Cold Lands

The polar regions are the coldest and bleakest places on Earth. Antarctica, around the South Pole, is mostly covered by thick ice, and fierce blizzards blow loose snow over the surface. Temperatures rarely rise above freezing point during the day and a world record −125°F has been recorded near the South Pole. No people live permanently in Antarctica, but some scientists work there in heated homes under the ice. Penguins live around the shores of Antarctica and the seas are rich in fish and whales.

Polar bears live on the ice floes of the Arctic Ocean, hunting seals and young walruses. And around the Arctic Ocean are parts of North America, Europe and Asia, called the *tundra*. Here the snow melts during the short summers, when temperatures may rise to 10°C. Flowering plants then carpet the ground, but it is too cold for trees. Migrating animals such as reindeer graze in the tundra. Arctic people include the Eskimos. They once lived by hunting. They built winter homes of ice called igloos, but most Eskimos now have modern homes.

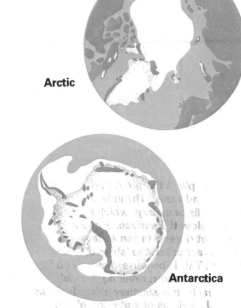

Arctic

Antarctica

Above: One map shows the ice-covered continent of Antarctica around the South Pole. The other map shows the region around the North Pole, which contains the icy Arctic Ocean. The northern parts of North America, Europe and Asia surround this ocean. These lands have long, cold winters, but plants grow in the short summers.

Below: Penguins gather in large colonies on the icy coasts of Antarctica. The emperor penguin hatches its egg on its feet and the young birds huddle together for warmth.

Most people in the great Sahara Desert live around oases. These fertile places have wells or springs which tap water in rocks below the surface. Some nomads cross hot deserts in camel caravans. Camels are called the 'ships of the desert'. This is because they can go long distances without drinking. But when they reach an oasis, they often drink up to 26 US gallons of water in only 10 minutes. The camel is suited to the desert in another way. A web of strong skin connects its two widely spaced toes and prevents its feet from sinking into the sand.

Many animals live in the desert despite the heat and the dryness. The smaller animals hide away during the day to escape the fierce sun and venture out at night. Many of them get the water they need from the seeds they eat.

Hot Deserts

Hot deserts cover about one-fifth of the world's land areas. They have mostly clear skies and high temperatures. The average rainfall is under 10 inches a year. Several years may pass with hardly any rain, then a thunderstorm may drench the land. Seeds which have been dormant for years rapidly germinate and many plants flower. When this happens in the Australian desert, people flock to the area to see this superb spectacle.

The world's largest desert is the Sahara in North Africa. It contains sand dunes, plains of loose gravel and bare, rocky uplands. Most plants in hot deserts, such as thorn bushes and cacti, are drought-resistant. The most useful desert animal is the camel. It can go for long periods without water. It loses weight, but regains it when it drinks. Deserts become fertile when they are irrigated (watered). Some deserts, like those of the Middle East, are rich in oil and natural gas. These fuels lie hidden far below the surface.

Penguins are awkward creatures on land, waddling around on their webbed feet. To move faster they slide on their bellies over the ice, pushing themselves along with their stubby wings. In the water penguins are fast and agile as they chase fish under water.

61

Grasslands

Tropical grasslands, called savanna, campos or llanos, occur north and south of the equator in Africa, South America, southern Asia and northern Australia. They are in warm regions with high rainfall. But, because they have a marked dry season, forests do not develop except in such areas as river valleys. Tropical grasslands are used for cattle rearing and some crop farming. But there is a danger that the winds will blow away the exposed soil in the dry season. Such soil erosion can make a region infertile in a few years. In Africa, the savanna supports many animals.

Temperate or mid-latitude grasslands have less rain and much colder winters than tropical grasslands. Trees are also rare on the dry, windswept plains. Huge areas of temperate grasslands, which are also called prairies, steppes or pampas, have become cattle ranches or vast wheat farms. The wildlife has been much reduced. In Australia, sheep have replaced most of the kangaroos and wallabies of the grasslands.

Above: Cattle ranching is a major activity in such savanna regions as East Africa.

Below: Temperate grasslands in North America have become leading wheat-growing regions. The land is flat and easy to farm.

Woods and Meadows

Moist temperate regions have some rain all the year round, with warm summers and fairly cold winters. Such regions once had huge forests of deciduous trees, such as ash, beech, chestnut, hickory, maple and oak. These trees shed their leaves in winter in order to protect themselves against the cold. Such forests once grew over most of western Europe, northern China and the eastern USA, areas which now contain some of the world's most densely populated regions. Most of these forests have been cut down. Their wood was used for building and as a fuel. In the USA, the forests largely vanished in about 300 years and the land was used for farming. The wildlife dwindled and soil erosion became a serious problem. This also happened on the lower slopes of the mountains of South Island, New Zealand. Britain's forests were replaced by a pleasant landscape of plowed fields, river meadows, hedgerows and occasional clumps of woodland. But the destruction of forests led to a great decline in wildlife.

Above: Forests once covered the moist temperate regions in the middle latitudes. In England, these forests have been replaced by a complicated patchwork of fields.

Below: Moist temperate regions in New Zealand support great numbers of sheep.

Northern Forests

Cold snowy climates are warmer than polar regions, but colder than temperate regions. Vast coniferous forests, called taiga, grow in cold snowy climates. Coniferous trees include birch, fir, pine and spruce. These cold forests are found only in the Northern Hemisphere. No large land masses in a similar latitude exist in the Southern Hemisphere.

Many furred animals, such as ermine, mink, otter and wolverine live in the forests. They have attracted hunters, who have greatly reduced the numbers of these animals. Larger animals include bears, bull moose, caribou, reindeer and wolves. Many trees in these cold forests are valuable softwoods. They are cut down and floated along rivers to sawmills. Sawn timber is used to make furniture and many other things. Many logs are made into wood pulp and paper. The northern forests do not contain many people, because of the cold weather and their generally infertile soils.

Above: The map shows the vast belt of cold coniferous forest that sprawls over North America, northern Europe and northern Asia. It lies south of the tundra and north of the deciduous forests and grassland.

Rain Forests

Rain forests grow in the tropics. Near the equator, there are areas which are hot and wet throughout the year. These regions support tall evergreen trees, such as ebony, mahogany and teak. The leaves of the trees block out sunlight from the muddy forest floor, so that few plants can grow there. The largest equatorial forests are in the Amazon basin of South America and the Zaire (or Congo) basin of Africa. Most wild animals live in the trees. Most people live in forest clearings. They grow food crops such as cassava, manioc and sweet potatoes. Large plantations produce cocoa, coffee, palm-oil, rubber and sugar-cane.

There are similar tropical forests in the monsoon lands of southern Asia and north-eastern Australia, where there is a dry season. But these forests are often less dense than equatorial forests. They also contain some trees that shed their leaves before the dry season in order to conserve water. Rice is the main food crop in monsoon lands. Equatorial and tropical forests are now being rapidly cut down.

Above: The map shows the world's rain forests, which grow in warm tropical regions. Below: The world's largest rain forest is in South America, in the Amazon River basin. It contains many animals, such as monkeys and colorful birds.

River Valleys

Rivers carry worn pieces of rock from their upper courses to the sea. As the rocks move along, they break down into smaller and smaller pieces. Finally, they become fine alluvium. This alluvium is spread over river valleys when rivers flood. It sometimes piles up in deltas, areas of new fertile land at the river mouths.

Fertile river valleys and deltas are the most densely populated regions on Earth. Farmers can produce large crops because of the rich soil and plentiful water. Some valleys have been centres of early civilizations. These include the valleys of the Tigris-Euphrates in Iraq, the Nile in Egypt, the Indus in Pakistan, the Ganges in India, and the various river valleys of eastern China.

Above: Rivers flow swiftly down their steep upper courses but they become slow-moving when they near the sea. The lower valleys and deltas of many rivers are thickly populated. In parts of China, including Hong Kong, people live on river boats called sampans, right.

Below: Buffalo plow the flooded 'paddy' fields in which rice is grown. Rice from the great river valleys is the staple diet of Asia.

Among the Mountains

Mountain regions are often remote, cold places, which are so difficult to climb and cross that they were once hide-outs for bandits. But they are also among the world's most beautiful places. They have varied scenery, because the higher one goes, the colder it gets. Temperatures fall by an average of 12°F for every 1,100 yards. High mountains near the equator have bands of vegetation ranging from rain forest at the bottom to polar climates on the ice-covered peaks.

Farmers often use high mountain pastures for summer grazing. For example, Swiss farmers live in sheltered mountain valleys in winter. In summer, they take their herds up to the high mountain slopes. To survive in mountains, animals must be able to move quickly over jagged slopes. One such animal is North America's bighorn, which is wonderfully sure-footed.

Below: The sure-footed bighorn is at home among the steepest crags of the Rocky Mountains.

Cattle graze on the flower-strewn Alpine meadows.

A World of Atoms

All substances that exist – human beings, animals, plants, wood, rocks, air, metals, water – are made up of matter. Wood is solid matter; water is liquid matter; and air is gaseous matter.

The smallest piece of a substance that is still recognizable as that substance is called a molecule. The molecule in turn is made up of a number of atoms. Different substances are made up of different kinds of atoms.

The simplest substances are those whose molecules are made up of just one kind of atom. They are called the chemical elements and can be regarded as the building blocks of matter. The metals iron, copper and gold are elements. So are carbon and oxygen.

Other substances have molecules made up of combinations of different atoms. They are called compounds. Atoms of iron, for example, combine with atoms of oxygen to form the compound iron oxide, or rust.

It was once thought that atoms were the smallest particles of matter that could exist – 100 million atoms, side by side, measure less than ½ inch! But we now know that atoms are made up of even smallest particles and we can even split them.

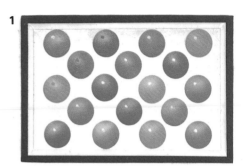

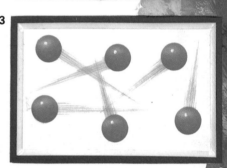

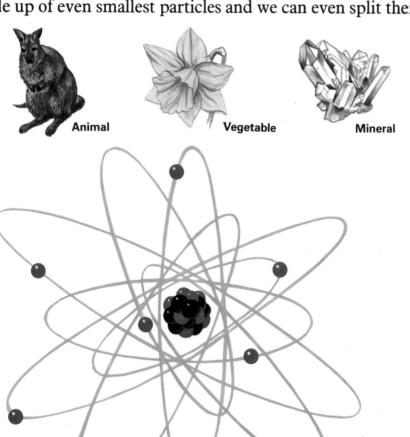

Animal **Vegetable** **Mineral**

Above: In a solid (1) the molecules are close together and attract one another strongly. They remain firmly in place. In a liquid (2) the molecules are farther apart. They still attract one another, but not strongly, and they are free to move around. So a liquid can flow. In a gas (3) the molecules are far apart and exert little attraction on one another. They travel very fast.

Left: All things on Earth, be they animal, vegetable or mineral, are made up of millions upon millions of atoms. Every atom is constructed in a similar way. The main part is the nucleus. This is made up of tiny particles called protons and neutrons. Around the nucleus circle a number of even tinier particles called electrons. There are as many electrons as there are protons. The protons have a positive electric charge and the electrons have a negative charge. So the atom as a whole is electrically neutral.

Below: The menacing cloud from an atomic-bomb explosion. An atomic explosion has many thousand times the destructive force of an ordinary explosion. It also produces deadly radiation and fallout. Fallout is dangerous radioactive dust carried by winds and falls far away from the site of the explosion.

Below: Energy is released when atoms split, or undergo fission. A uranium atom may undergo fission when it is bombarded by a neutron. It splits into two, releasing energy as light, heat and radiation. Two or more neutrons are also produced in the process. These neutrons may in turn go on to cause fission in other atoms, causing what is called a chain reaction. The energy released when a chain reaction occurs is enormous.

Bottom: The chain reaction is a useful source of power when it can be controlled. This is done in a nuclear reactor. In a reactor, the core contains the uranium 'fuel'. The chain reaction is controlled by means of control rods. A liquid or gas coolant circulates through the core and extracts heat. It gives up this heat to water in a heat exchanger. The steam produced then goes to turbine generating machinery.

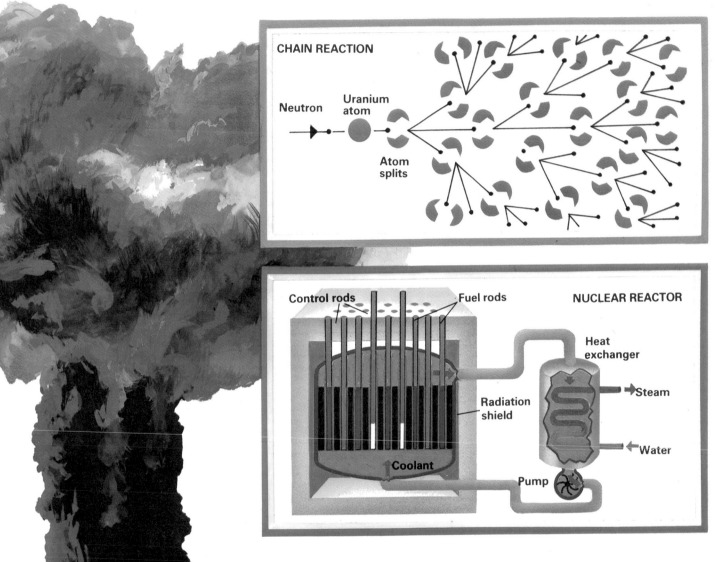

CHAIN REACTION

Neutron · Uranium atom · Atom splits

NUCLEAR REACTOR

Control rods · Fuel rods · Heat exchanger · Steam · Radiation shield · Water · Coolant · Pump

NUCLEAR FUSION

Fission is a nuclear process that occurs when very heavy atoms, such as uranium, split. The opposite kind of process can also occur. Very light atoms can combine to form heavier ones. This process is called fusion. Fusion also releases enormous amounts of energy.

It is in fact fusion that provides the energy to make the Sun and the stars shine. Inside the Sun, at temperatures of millions of degrees, atoms of hydrogen combine, or fuse together, to form atoms of helium.

Scientists on Earth have imitated this process and produced the hydrogen bomb, the most terrible weapon of all. They are now trying to find ways of controlling fusion to produce useful power. They are trying to do this in two ways – with powerful magnetic machines called tokamaks, and with lasers.

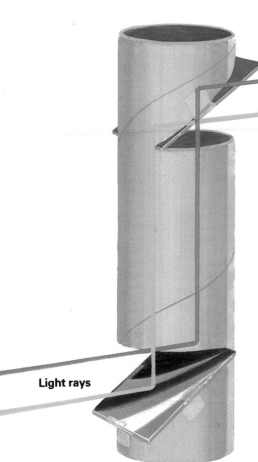

Light rays

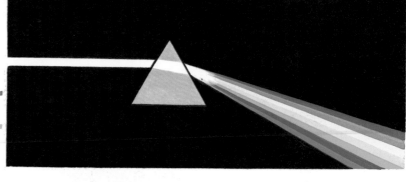

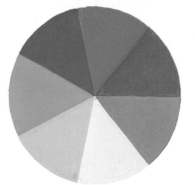

Left: You can use the property of mirrors to reflect light to help you make a periscope. Fix the mirrors in the tube exactly at an angle of 45°. Then you will be able to see over walls and look round corners.

Above: Ordinary white light from the Sun is actually a mixture of many different colors. You can show this by passing a beam of sunlight through a wedge of glass (a prism). The light emerges as a much broader beam, which forms a band (spectrum) showing all the colors of the rainbow. You can turn these colors back into white by means of a color wheel. Paint the colors on the wheel as shown. Then spin it and watch the colors merge together to form white.

Simple Science

If you hold a pea in one hand and a golf ball in the other, and drop them, which hits the ground first? You will probably say 'the golf ball'. Try the experiment yourself, and you will be astonished to observe that both pea and golf ball hit the ground at exactly the same time!

If you measure the time they take to fall and the distance they fall, you can work out how much they accelerate under the pull of the Earth, or gravity. By carrying out this simple experiment and observing what happens, you have increased your knowledge of the world around you. You have been practising science.

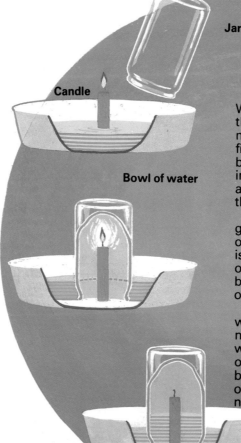

Jar

Candle

Bowl of water

HOW MUCH OXYGEN?

We are able to live on Earth because the air contains oxygen which we must breathe to remain alive. You can find the amount of oxygen in the air by a simple experiment. Fix a candle in a bowl of water. Light the candle, and then place a jar over it down into the water. Watch what happens.

The water level inside the jar gradually rises. This shows that some of the air is being used up, and water is taking its place. In fact it is the oxygen in the air that is being used up because substances combine with oxygen when they burn.

Soon the candle goes out and the water level remains steady. Make a note of where the water level is. You will find that it has gone about one-fifth of the way up the jar. This is because air contains about one-fifth oxygen. Most of the other gas is nitrogen.

Every day of our lives we benefit from the knowledge gained by careful observation and experiment by dedicated men and women of science down the ages. One of the first true scientists was Galileo in the 1600s, who first carried out experiments with falling bodies like the one described.

There are two broad scientific fields – the physical sciences and the biological, or life sciences. The main physical sciences are physics and chemistry. Physics deals with such things as energy and forces, including light, heat and magnetism. Chemistry is concerned with the way substances are made up and how they react together. The biological sciences include zoology and botany. Zoology is the study of animals, while botany is the study of plants.

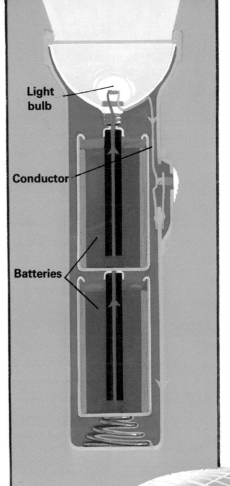

Light bulb

Conductor

Batteries

LIGHT BULB
The electricity flows into the light bulb and passes through a thin wire, or filament. It causes the filament to become white hot and thus give out light. The wire is made from a metal called tungsten which can resist the heat without breaking or melting.

CONDUCTORS
Brass strips carry the current from the battery to the bulb. Like most metals, brass is a good conductor of electricity. The rest of the torch is often made from plastic or rubber, which do not conduct electricity. They are insulators.

BATTERIES
In a torch battery, or dry cell, the electricity is produced by chemical action. This takes place between two electrodes and a paste containing ammonium chloride. The electrodes are a carbon rod (in the middle) and zinc, which forms the battery container.

Iron and a few metals like it are different from other metals because they can be magnetized – they can be made into magnets. Magnetism is a strange kind of force that we cannot see or feel, but we can see it in action. A horseshoe magnet, for example, readily attracts objects made from iron. But it will not attract objects made from aluminum or copper.

The magnetism in an object, say a bar, is not the same all over. It appears to be concentrated at the ends, at points we call the poles. The poles at each end are different from one another. When a bar magnet is suspended, one end always points north, the other south.

A suspended magnet (a compass) points north-south because the Earth itself acts like a magnet. And the magnet aligns itself with invisible lines of the Earth's magnetic force. But magnetic north-south differs slightly from 'true' north-south shown on maps.

If a south pole of one magnet is brought near the south pole of another, they push each other away. But if a north pole and a south pole come together, they attract one another.

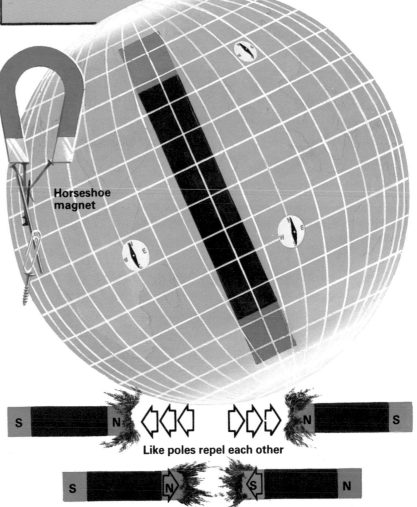

Horseshoe magnet

Like poles repel each other

Unlike poles attract each other

71

Energy and Power

Oil drill pipe

Oil rig

Gas

Oil

Wa[ter]

Warm swamps covered many regions of the Earth some 300 million years ago (main picture). In them grew huge ferns and horsetails. When these plants died, they fell into the swamp and began to decay. Over the years the remains dried and hardened into coal, now found sandwiched between the rock layers (inset above). The organisms that lived in ancient seas also died and decayed, and we find their remains today as oil and natural gas, trapped in the rock layers (inset below).

We could not live the way we do today without a plentiful supply of energy. Most of the energy we use comes from oil, coal and natural gas. These are known as fossil fuels because they are the remains of organisms – plants and animals – that once lived. And they are burned to release their energy.

Most oil, or gasoline, is made into fuels that are burned in engines, to power cars, trucks, locomotives and airplanes. These fuels include gasoline, kerosene and diesel oil. Most coal is burned in power stations to produce electricity. The heat from the burning coal heats water in a boiler into steam. The steam then spins a turbine, which in turn spins a generator to make electricity. Electricity is a very convenient way of 'carrying' energy from place to place.

Some power stations use another kind of 'fuel' to produce heat for the boilers. This is nuclear fuel, such as uranium. Under certain conditions uranium atoms can be made to

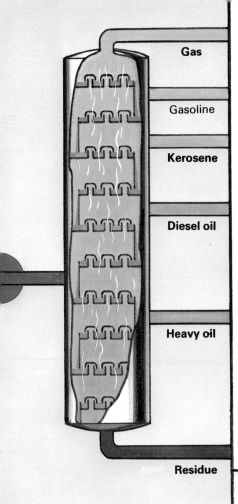

Gas

Gasoline

Kerosene

Diesel oil

Heavy oil

Residue

split, and this releases large amounts of heat (see page 69). There are now some 200 nuclear power stations around the world.

Alternative Energy Sources

Supplies of fossil fuels and uranium are obtained from the ground. Eventurally these supplies will run out. Then we must find alternative sources of energy. We are already using one – flowing water. We harness this power in hydro-electric ('water-electric') schemes. The water spins water turbines, which drive the electricity generators.

Schemes to harness other natural energy sources are also well under way. Engineers are building huge wind turbines, wave-power devices and solar 'power towers'.

Left: Before it can be used, crude oil must be refined, or processed, in an oil refinery. The first stage is distillation, which takes place in this kind of tower. Oil vapor passes through the tower, and the various substances it contains separate out into various parts, or fractions.

Below: Some regions of the world are blessed with plenty of sunshine, a 'free' source of energy waiting to be tapped. This can be done with a solar power tower. Large numbers of mirrors reflect sunshine onto a boiler at the top of a tower. This heats water in the boiler into steam.

Great Inventions

The story of civilization can be traced in the inventions that Man has made. Among the early inventions of greatest importance were metal smelting, in the 4000s BC; the wheel and the plow, in the 3000s BC; and the harnessing of water power, in Roman times. But the pace of invention was slow until the 1400s, the time of the Renaissance, or 'rebirth of learning'.

Hot air balloon, 1783

1450	**Printing Press** Johannes Gutenberg, Germany
1590	**Compound Microscope** Zacharias Janssen, the Netherlands
1608/9	**Refracting Telescope** Hans Lippershey, the Netherlands, and Galileo Galilei, Italy
1668	**Reflecting Telescope** Isaac Newton, Britain
1698	**Steam Pump** Thomas Savery, Britain
1712	**Beam Engine** Thomas Newcomen, Britain
1733	**Flying Shuttle** John Kay, Britain
1767	**Spinning Jenny** James Hargreaves, Britain
1780s	**Improved Steam Engine** James Watt, Britain
1783	**Hot-air Balloon** Montgolfier Brothers, France
1785	**Power Loom** Edmund Cartwright, Britain
1792	**Cotton Gin** Eli Whitney, United States
1800	**Electric Battery** Allessandro Volta, Italy
1800	**Lathe** Henry Maudslay, Britain
1804	**Steam Locomotive** Richard Trevithick, Britain
1815	**Safety Lamp** Humphry Davy, Britain
1815	**Stethoscope** René T. H. Laënec, France
1836	**Revolver** Samuel Colt, United States
1837	**Telegraph** William Cooke and Charles Wheatstone, Britain; Samuel Morse, United States
1839	**Steam Hammer** James Nasmyth, Britain
1845	**Sewing Machine** Elias Howe, United States
1856	**Bessemer Process** Henry Bessemer, Britain

1867	**Dynamite** Alfred Nobel, Sweden
1872	**Typewriter** Christopher L. Scholes, United States
1876	**Telephone** Alexander Graham Bell, United States
1877	**Phonograph (Gramophone)** Thomas Alva Edison, United States
1878	**Cathode-ray Tube** William Crookes, Britain
1878/9	**Electric Lamp** Joseph Swan, Britain, and Thomas Alva Edison, United States
1880s	**Machine Gun** Hiram Stevens Maxim, United States
1884	**Steam Turbine** Charles Algernon Parsons, Britain
1885	**Gasoline Engine** Karl Benz and Gottlieb Daimler, Germany
1888	**Pneumatic Tyre** John Boyd Dunlop, Britain
1892	**Diesel Engine** Rudolf Diesel, Germany
1895	**Radio** Guglielmo Marconi, Italy
1903	**Powered Aircraft** Wilbur and Orville Wright, United States
1926	**Television** John Logie Baird, Britain, and Vladimir Zworykin, United States
1930	**Jet Engine** Frank Whittle, Britain
1944	**Digital Computer** Howard Aiken, United States
1947	**Polaroid Camera** Edwin H. Land, United States
1955	**Hovercraft** Christopher Cockerell, Britain
1971	**Microprocessor** Intel Corporation, United States

The wheel was invented about 3000 BC

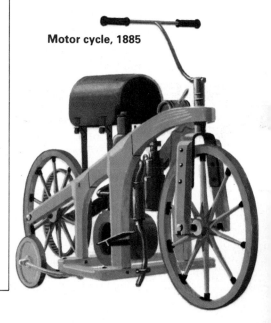

Motor cycle, 1885

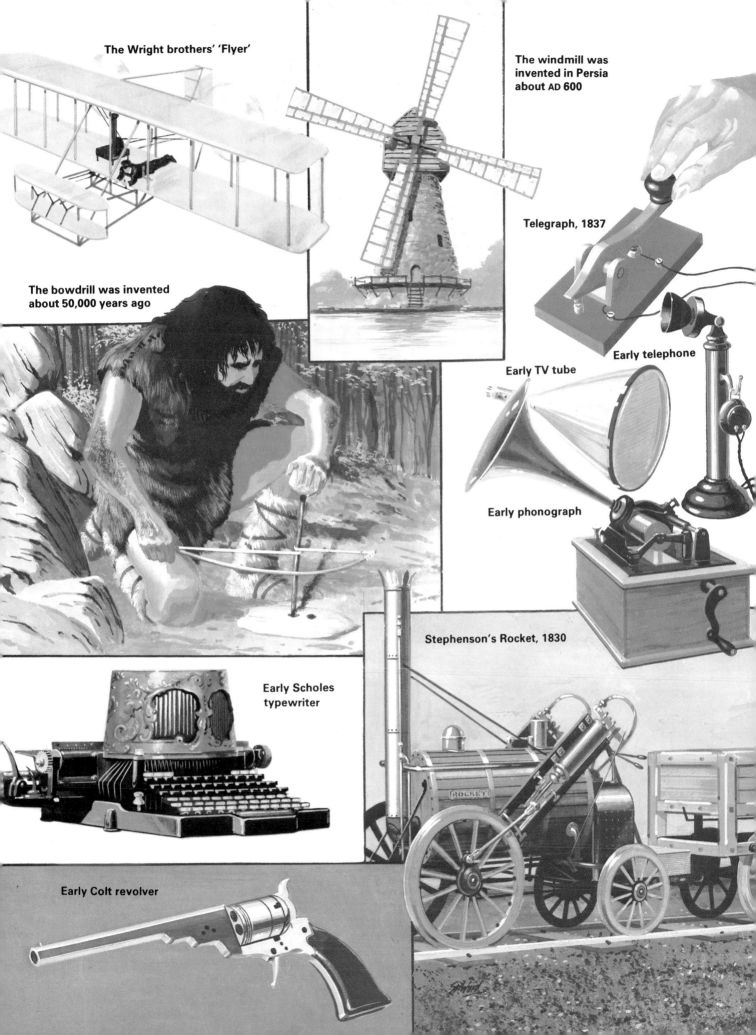

The Wright brothers' 'Flyer'

The windmill was invented in Persia about AD 600

Telegraph, 1837

The bowdrill was invented about 50,000 years ago

Early telephone

Early TV tube

Early phonograph

Stephenson's Rocket, 1830

Early Scholes typewriter

Early Colt revolver

Ships and the Sea

People first went down to the sea in ships about 7,000 years ago. Since then the seas have provided a major 'highway' for trade between countries. They have also been a battleground on which nations have won and lost empires.

Until the 1800s sails provided the main means of propelling ships. The most magnificent sailing ships were the swift and graceful clippers, which carried tea and later wool between the Far East and Europe. They were full-rigged ships with a huge sail area on three tall masts. In favorable conditions they could reach a speed of 20 knots (23 mph).

The Age of Steam

However, even while the clippers were setting new records in the mid-1800s, the days of sail were numbered. The future lay in the new steamships which were beginning to cross the Atlantic Ocean. In 1845 the 'Great Britain' showed

SHIPS THROUGH THE AGES
(drawn to scale)

Medieval merchant 'cog'

Ancient Egyptian trading ship

the way ahead. It was an iron steamship propelled by screw propeller. Within a few years metal hulls and screw propellers were standard.

The early steamships had piston steam engines, similar to those used in factories. In the 1890s a new steam 'engine' showed its superiority – the steam-turbine. Steam turbines still power most large ships. Many smaller ships have diesel engines similar to those in trucks, only much bigger.

A handful of ships are nuclear powered. They are mainly naval ships, such as aircraft carriers and submarines. Nuclear power has not yet proved economical enough for merchant ships.

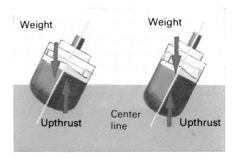

Above: Two main forces act on a ship floating in the water. One is its weight, which acts downwards. The other is an upward force, or upthrust. Ship designers design a ship so that the weight and upthrust act so as to right the vessel when it rolls (left). In a bad design (right) the weight and upthrust act so as to roll the vessel further and make it capsize.

Bottom: An interesting comparison of the sizes of ships through the ages. The 'Atlantic' is a giant supertanker and, with a length of 1,330 feet, is one of the largest ships now afloat. It transports crude oil from the Middle East oilfields.

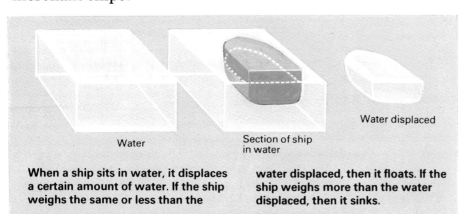

Water

Section of ship in water

Water displaced

When a ship sits in water, it displaces a certain amount of water. If the ship weighs the same or less than the water displaced, then it floats. If the ship weighs more than the water displaced, then it sinks.

Mid-19th century clipper

Mid-19th century steamship

1980 Esso 'Atlantic', 1,330 feet

The Story of Railways

Stephenson's Rocket opened the Liverpool and Manchester Railway in 1830.

The birth of the railways as we know them today can be traced to 1825. In that year George Stephenson built the world's first public railway, the Stockton and Darlington line, in northern England. He also built steam locomotives to run on it, beginning a revolution in transport that spread like wildfire throughout the world.

Goodbye to Steam

The age of steam on the railways lasted in most countries until the 1950s. Since then steam locomotives have been replaced by diesel and electric locomotives. Steam locomotives were magnificent machines and exciting to watch. But they were very inefficient, dirty and noisy.

The modern diesel and electric locomotives, on the other hand, are efficient, clean and quiet. They can also accelerate more quickly and have a higher top speed. The fastest diesel is British Rail's High Speed Train, which holds the world diesel record of 143 mph.

A French electric TGV (Train à Grand Vitesse) holds the absolute rail speed record, with a speed of no less then 236 mph. The TGVs now run on the Paris to Lyons line, specially built flat and straight for maximum speed. The other outstanding high-speed railway, the Shinkansen in Japan, also runs on specially built track.

In Canada, Italy, Spain and Britain railway engineers are experimenting with tilting body designs to allow high speeds on existing curved track.

Above: 'Ellerman Lines', a preserved steam locomotive of the Merchant Navy class, built for mainline service in Britain in the 1950s. Weighing some 96 tons, it is a Pacific, or 4-6-2 type, having a 4-wheeled bogie in front, 6 driving wheels and 2 wheels beneath the cab. Preservation societies now exist in many countries to restore steam locomotives to their former splendor.

Right: An example of a different kind of railway track, a monorail ('single-rail'). In this particular design, found at Tokyo Zoo, the passenger car is suspended from a wheeled trolley that runs along the overhead rail. In other kinds of monorails, the passenger car straddles the track.

Below: A conventional twin-rail track. The rails are clamped firmly to the sleepers, which are embedded in stone ballast. These days the rails are laid in very long lengths, made by welding short rails together.

Rail

Steel clip

Sleepers

Ballast

Below: Currently the fastest trains in service are the TGVs, which run between Paris and Lyons in France. Like all the latest high speed trains, the TGVs are highly streamlined. They operate at speeds up to 160 mph. They are designed as a complete unit, with two power cars and eight trailer cars making up each trainset.

SNCF

The Automobile

1902 Panhard Levassor

1909 Rolls-Royce 'Silver Ghost'

1930 Aston Martin

1960 BMC 'Mini'

1982 BMW Mi Coupé

In 1885 a new type of vehicle appeared on the roads in Stuttgart, Germany. It looked much like some of the small steam carriages seen in other towns. But it differed in one important respect – its engine used gasoline as fuel. It was the ancestor of the modern automobile. Its inventor was named Karl Benz.

In less than a century the automobile has developed into our most important form of transport, which greatly affects the way we live. Something like 200 million automobiles now travel on the world's roads. The latest ones are sleek vehicles, carefully streamlined so that they slip through the air easily. Some are designed for speed, being able to travel over 124 mph. Others are designed for economy, being able to travel over 45 miles on a US galon of gasoline. Many are built with the aid of robots.

Automobiles are a very comfortable and convenient form of transport, but they have their disadvantages. They cause accidents; they burn a fuel obtained from oil, which will soon be in short supply, and they are a major source of pollution. For these reasons automobile manufacturers are continually redesigning their autos to make them safer, use less fuel, and cause less pollution. They are also experimenting with new kinds of engines that run on steam, hot air, and electricity. These should cause no pollution at all.

THE FOUR-STROKE CYCLE

Below: Most automobile engines are piston engines. They contain pistons that move up and down in cylinders. A mixture of gasoline and air is burned in the cylinders to produce hot gases. The gases expand and force the pistons down the cylinders to produce power to move the vehicle. The diagram shows how the fuel mixture is taken into the cylinders (1), compressed (2,) burned (3), and removed (4), according to a regular cycle, called the four-stroke cycle.

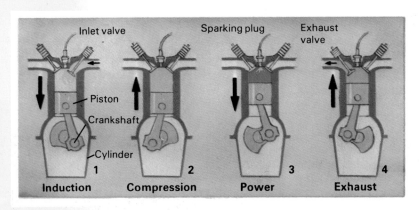

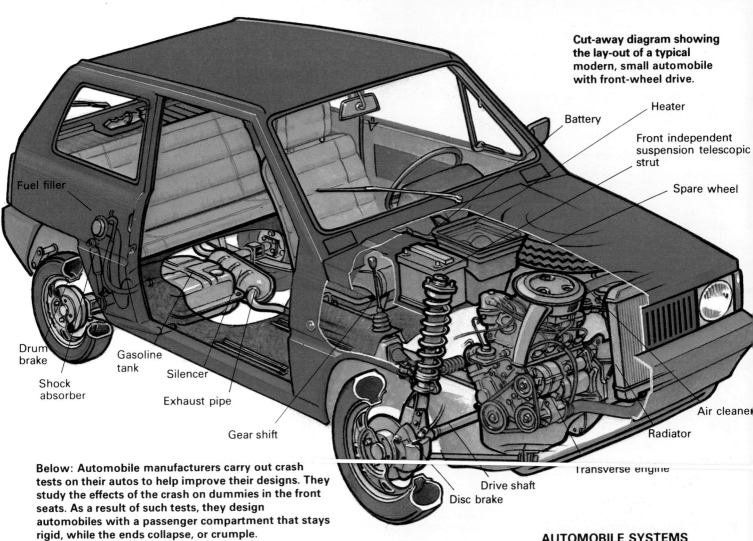

Cut-away diagram showing the lay-out of a typical modern, small automobile with front-wheel drive.

Battery

Heater

Front independent suspension telescopic strut

Spare wheel

Fuel filler

Drum brake

Shock absorber

Gasoline tank

Silencer

Exhaust pipe

Gear shift

Air cleaner

Radiator

Drive shaft

Disc brake

Transverse engine

Below: Automobile manufacturers carry out crash tests on their autos to help improve their designs. They study the effects of the crash on dummies in the front seats. As a result of such tests, they design automobiles with a passenger compartment that stays rigid, while the ends collapse, or crumple.

Crumple zone

Crumple zone

AUTOMOBILE SYSTEMS

An automobile is a most complicated piece of machinery, made up of over 10,000 different parts. For simplicity we can group these parts into a number of different systems. Each system plays a particular part in the operation of the car.

THE ENGINE changes the energy in the fuel into mechanical motion.

THE TRANSMISSION SYSTEM carries, or transmits, the motion from the engine to the wheels. It consists usually of a clutch, gearbox, propeller shaft, and a final drive on the driving wheel axle.

THE STEERING SYSTEM allows the driver to turn the front wheels and so steer the automobile.

THE BRAKING SYSTEM gives the driver the power to slow down and stop the automobile.

THE SUSPENSION SYSTEM of springs and shock absorbers cushions the passenger from the effects of bumpy roads.

THE ELECTRICAL SYSTEM provides electricity from a battery to make sparks to ignite the fuel and power the lights, instruments, horn and other equipment.

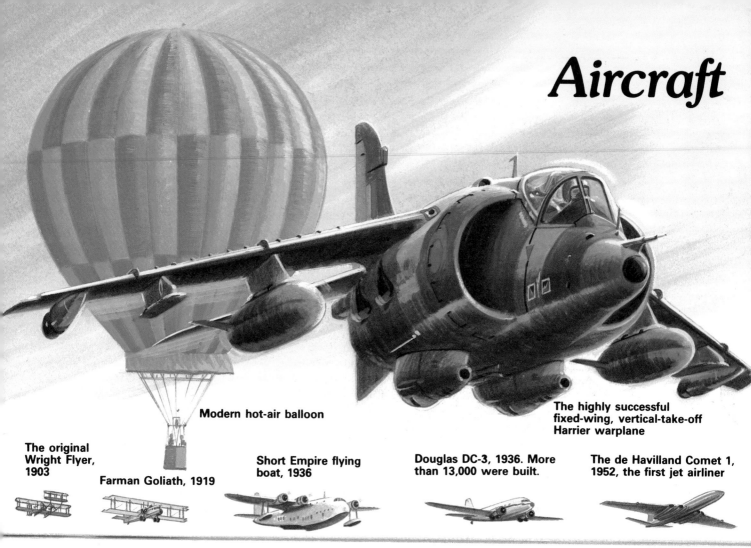

Aircraft

Modern hot-air balloon

The highly successful fixed-wing, vertical-take-off Harrier warplane

The original Wright Flyer, 1903

Farman Goliath, 1919

Short Empire flying boat, 1936

Douglas DC-3, 1936. More than 13,000 were built.

The de Havilland Comet 1, 1952, the first jet airliner

The story of Man's conquest of the air began almost exactly two centuries ago, in 1783. In June of that year two French brothers, Joseph and Etienne Montgolfier, launched a hot-air balloon. But such balloons are now used only for sport. Today the skies belong to the airplane, commonly just called plane.

The first plane flight took place on 17 December 1903, at Kitty Hawk in North Carolina, in the United States. The plane was built by the Wright brothers, Orville and Wilbur. The first flight lasted for a mere 12 seconds, but it showed the way ahead. In 1909 Louis Blériot flew across the English Channel; ten years later John Alcock and Arthur Whitten Brown made the first non-stop flight across the Atlantic Ocean.

The Coming of the Airliner

During the 1920s and 1930s regular, or scheduled flights began, at first carrying airmail and later passengers. This was the era of the flying boat. By the end of the 1930s, as the world headed into World War II, a new type of plane was being developed: the jet. After the war the jet plane came into its own, first as a fighter, then as a commercial airliner.

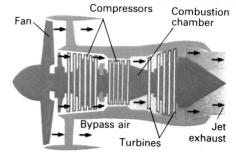

Above: A turbofan engine, used in most airliners. Air is taken into the engine and compressed. Fuel is burned in the compressed air in the combustion chamber. The hot gases produced spin the turbines before emerging as a jet. The by-pass air helps make the jet more efficient.

Below: A plane gets its 'lift' from the shape of its wings, a shape known as an aerofoil.

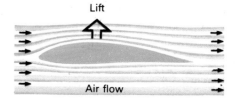

82

VERTICAL TAKE-OFF

One drawback of the ordinary plane is that it needs a long runway for taking off and landing. Over the years, different types of aircraft have been developed to overcome this drawback. The most successful has been the helicopter, developed in the 1930s, mainly by Igor Sikorsky in the United States. The helicopter obtains its lift by whirling blades on top of its fuselage. The only successful vertical-take-off and landing (VTOL) fixed-wing plane has been the Harrier fighter (left). This moves vertically up and down by deflecting the jet exhausts from its engines.

In the 1960s jet planes became faster and bigger. In 1969 came the maiden flight of the supersonic airliner Concorde, developed jointly by Britain and France. It is still the fastest airliner in service, being capable of a speed of some 1,400 mph. This is twice the speed of sound, and is faster than a rifle bullet.

In the same year came the maiden flight of the Boeing 747, the first of the big passenger jets, known as jumbo jets. The Boeing 747 can carry 400 passengers or more, but can operate efficiently only when most seats are filled. Its four engines use a lot of fuel. In recent years, as fuel costs have risen sharply, smaller planes have been developed for more economical airline operation. They include the European Airbus and the Boeing 757 and 767, which all have two highly efficient turbofan engines.

The Anglo-French Concorde supersonic airliner, 1976

The Boeing 747, 1970, the first 'jumbo' jet

Most planes are equipped with an instrument landing system (ILS). This enables a pilot to position the plane accurately for a perfect landing on the runway. It works by means of radio beams.

BAE 146

Glide-path beacon

Localizer beacon

Runway

Inner marker

Middle marker

Outer marker

Rockets and Launchers

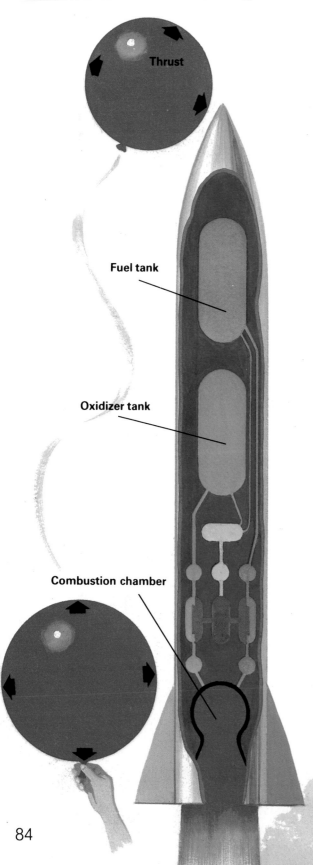

Thrust

Fuel tank

Oxidizer tank

Combustion chamber

Among the most powerful of all engines are the rockets used to launch satellites into space. Yet these rockets work on the same principle as the simple stick rockets we enjoy as fireworks. A fuel is burned in the rocket to produce hot gases, which are then allowed to escape through a nozzle. As the gases shoot backwards, the rocket is thrust forwards.

The substance that propels a rocket is called a propellant. Firework rockets use gunpowder. Space rockets use liquid propellants, such as liquid hydrogen (fuel) and liquid oxygen. They are much more powerful than solid propellants. Because rockets carry oxygen to burn their fuel, they can work in space, where there is no air.

Even so, a single liquid rocket cannot get into space by itself. It has to be helped on its way by other rockets. This is the idea behind the step rocket.

It is a launcher made up of several rockets joined end to end. The bottom rocket fires first and then falls away; the next rocket fires and falls away, and so on. The launcher gets faster and lighter each time and in this way can pick up enough speed to get into orbit.

Left: The essential parts of a liquid-propellant rocket. The propellants are pumped into the combustion chamber and burned. The hot gases produced escape from the nozzle and propel the rocket forwards.

Far left: The action of the balloon can explain how rocket propulsion works. When the balloon is blown up and held (bottom), the pressure on the inside is equal everywhere. When you let go the balloon (top), air escapes backwards through the neck. But the forward pressure remains and propels the balloon. A similar thing happens when the gases escape from a rocket nozzle.

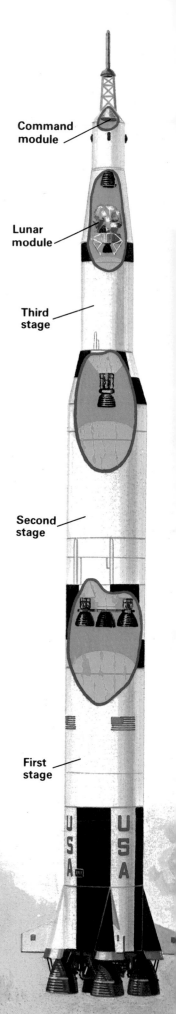

Command module

Lunar module

Third stage

Second stage

First stage

Left: This is the Saturn V/Apollo launcher, the biggest rocket ever launched by America. It was used in the 1960s and 1970s to send astronauts to the Moon. On the launch pad it stood no less than 364 feet high. All that eventually came back to Earth in one piece was the tiny command module containing the three man crew.

Below: In orbit the space shuttle orbiter opens its cargo-bay doors and launches a satellite.

Space Shuttle

On April 12, 1981, a new type of space launcher soared into the heavens. It was the American space shuttle. Unlike the launchers before it, the shuttle is a re-usable launch system. It consists of three main parts.

The most important part is the orbiter, which carries the crew. It looks much like a plane and is about the same size as a medium-range airliner like the DC-9. It is some 120 feet long and has a wing-span of some 75 feet. It has three powerful main rocket engines.

The orbiter rides into space on a huge tank, which carries liquid fuel for the main engines. On the launch pad, two solid rocket boosters are attached to the tank. The boosters and the orbiter's main engines all fire together at lift-off. Then the boosters fall away and parachute back to Earth to be used again. Later the fuel tank falls away, but it is not recovered. It is the only part of the shuttle 'stack' that is wasted.

Left: The shuttle blasts off the launch pad in a spectacular fireworks display. In a little over 10 minutes the orbiter is in orbit, travelling at 17,400 mph. It has discarded its fuel tank and rocket boosters.

Above: The orbiter takes off like a rocket, but lands like a glider. When it drops from orbit, it is travelling very fast indeed. Gradually the air slows it down to a safe landing speed, and it touches down on an ordinary runway.

Superstructures

Man has been a builder since the early days of civilization, and his structures have come to dominate the face of the Earth. Among the most impressive are skyscrapers and suspension bridges. They are examples of the work of the civil, or construction engineer. He also builds tunnels and dams. Some of his dams, too, are massive and, with skyscrapers and bridges, are often called superstructures. The most famous of all skyscrapers is the 1,040 feet high Empire State Building in New York City, completed in 1931. New York now has many other skyscrapers, including the taller World Trade Center (1,350 feet high). Skyscrapers can be built relatively easily in New York because there is solid rock just beneath the surface. This provides firm support, or foundation, for them.

Other cities are not so fortunate, so a different kind of foundation must be used. It is usually a pile foundation. Piles are long tubes of steel and concrete which are driven deep into the ground. A big concrete platform, or raft, is then usually built on top of the piles, and the skyscraper is built up from this. It is constructed with a strong frame of steel girders. The walls do not take the weight as they do in an ordinary building.

Below: Examples of Man's constructional skills – skyscrapers (left), oil rigs (centre) and dams. The three buildings shown, drawn to scale, represent great landmarks in construction. The Great Pyramid in Egypt is 480 feet high and was built in about 2580 BC. It remained the world's tallest structure for some 3800 years. The 985 foot Eiffel Tower in Paris was completed in 1889. Currently the world's highest building is the Sears Tower in Chicago, which soars to a fantastic 1450 feet.

Left: The Opera House in Sydney, Australia, is one of the most easily recognizable buildings in the world. Its roof is made up of a series of arch-like concrete shells. Queen Elizabeth II opened the Sydney Opera House in 1973, some 15 years after construction began.

Right: The suspension cables on the famous Golden Gate Bridge in San Francisco go up and over towers 745 feet high. Opened in 1937, the bridge has a centre span of 4200 feet. Until 1964 this was the longest bridge span in the world.

Since 1981, the Humber Bridge in England has been the world's longest-span (4,620 feet) bridge. Like most other long-span bridges it is a suspension bridge. In a suspension bridge, the bridge deck hangs, or is suspended, from thick steel cables. They are made up of tens of thousands of miles of thin steel wires bound together.

The cables go up and over tall towers on either side of the gap to be spanned. They are anchored firmly at each end. In the largest suspension bridges, the towers have to be built slightly out of parallel to allow for the curve of the Earth!

TYPES OF BRIDGE

Beam bridge

Arch bridge

Suspension bridge

Amazing Machines

Man is not a very strong creature, yet he can move mountains. He has no wings, yet he can fly. He cannot breathe under water, yet he can venture into the ocean deeps. He can even beat the pull of gravity and travel into space, surviving there for months at a time, and return safely. He can do these things – and many more – because he has the brain power to invent machines.

The modern Age of Machines began in the 1700s when several people invented machines to speed up textile making. Then a reliable steam engine was developed to run the machines. This mechanization led to a great change in the way things were made – to an Industrial Revolution.

At the present time we are in the grips of another industrial revolution, brought about by what is called automation. This means the use of machines that work automatically, with little need for human workers. The 'brains' behind the operation of these machines are the 'electronic brains' of the most amazing machine of all – the computer.

UNDERSTANDING THE COMPUTER

The ordinary computer is properly called a digital computer, because it handles data in the form of numbers, or digits. It does not use ordinary decimal digits (0–9), but just the two digits 1 and 0. These are called binary digits, or *bits.*

So all instructions and data must thus be coded into bits before the computer can work on them. The computer does most of this coding itself. But first the computer operator writes his instructions, or program, in a simplified 'language' that the computer can 'understand'. It is called a computer language.

The program and data form what is called the software of the computer. The computer equipment is called the hardware. The software is fed into the computer through an input device such as a keyboard or a magnetic disc or tape unit. Inside the computer it is stored in a memory unit. Calculations are carried out by an arithmetic unit under the control of a control unit. After calculations have been completed, the control unit directs the results to an output device. This may be a video display unit (VDU) like a television screen, or it may be a high-speed printer.

The word computer means calculator. And whatever job they do, computers work by carrying out a series of simple arithmetic calculations on sets of numbers. The numbers can represent all kinds of different information, or *data.* Computers are so marvellous because they can carry out such calculations at incredible speed, often performing hundreds of thousands of operations every second. But they cannot 'think' for themselves. They need a human being to tell them what to do.

How a hovercraft works

Fans blast air downwards

Flexible 'skirt' holds in air

Cushion of air

The hovercraft is equally at home on water as on land, gliding along on a cushion of air. It makes an excellent amphibious landing craft for the armed services. The largest hovercraft, such as the SRN4, are used as car ferries across the English Channel.

Right: The laser produces a narrow beam of pure light containing immense energy. It can be focused into a point of intense heat that can slice through metal like a knife through butter. Lasers have many other uses in the modern world from guiding tunnelling machines to 'playing' the latest compact record discs.

Left: Among the most powerful man-made machines are the turbogenerators used at power stations to produce electricity. The picture shows a massive generator rotor for a hydro-electric power plant.

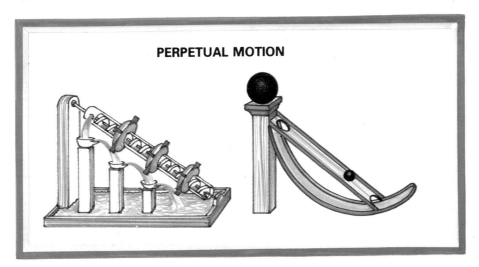

PERPETUAL MOTION

Many people have tried to invent machines that, once set moving, would carry on moving by themselves, in endless, or perpetual, motion. The pictures show two ideas. The Archimedean screw raises water as it turns. At the top the water spills out and cascades downwards and turns paddle wheels that turn the screw. It does not work because too much energy is lost in friction. In the ball-and-magnet machine, the idea is that the magnet attracts the ball up the slope. Near the top, the ball falls through the hole and back to the bottom, and is attracted up again. The drawback is that the magnet attracts the ball directly to it.

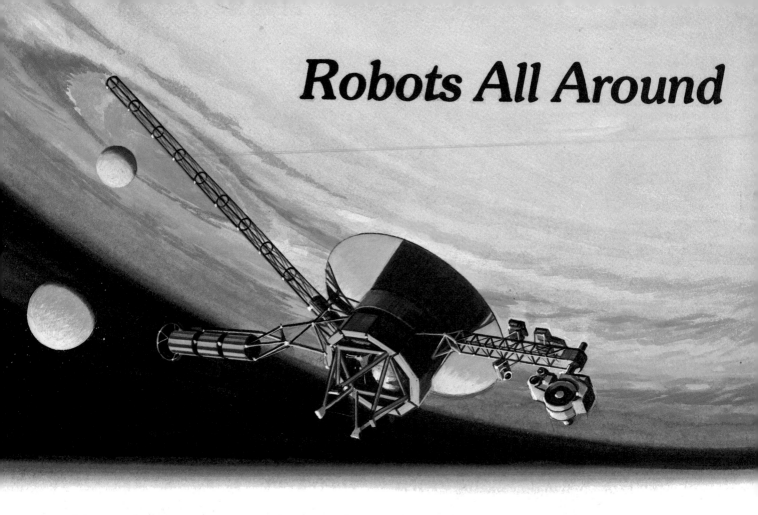

Robots All Around

We are now living in a world in which robots are taking over much of the work. Robots make our automobiles, fly our planes, work out our salaries, and prepare our accounts.

But these robots are not mechanical men and women. They do not look like us. They are machines specially built to do some of the things that human beings can. And they are given whatever shape is most suitable. Robots that are built to look like human beings are called androids. These are the kind that usually feature in science-fiction films and comics.

Although they may not look like us, robots need some human features in order to be able to do human work. First and foremost they need some kind of brain. Their 'brain' is a computer, which has a memory to remember instructions and the ability to control other equipment. It is itself a robot machine.

Another essential feature of many robots is an arm that can do the kind of things human beings can with their arms. One-armed robots are now coming into widespread use in industry. They are being used, for example, on car assembly lines. There they are used for welding car bodies and for paint spraying.

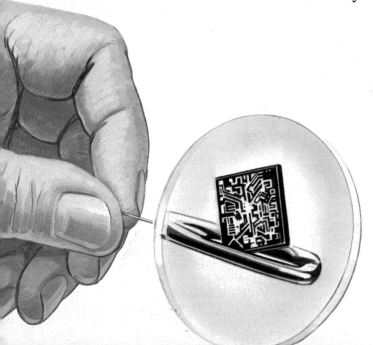

Below: A tiny crystal wafer provides the 'brainpower' for the new generation of robots. It is the silicon chip, which is so tiny that it can pass through the eye of a needle. Although it is so small, it contains thousands of electronic parts, which turn it into a powerful computer. It can 'remember' instructions given to it and guide the actions of a robot.

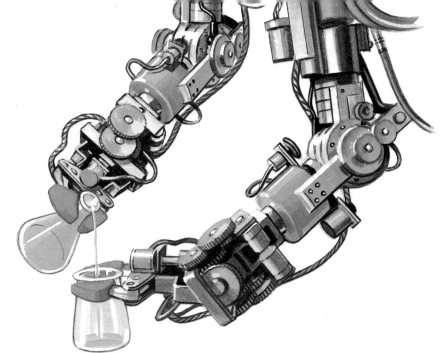

Right: It is very difficult to build a robot arm that works as well as the human arm. Many electric motors, joints and levers are required to imitate the actions of the human muscles, elbow, wrist, knuckles and fingers. Usually, however, robot arms do not need to be quite so complicated.

Opposite: Robot spacecraft, or probes, venture into the depths of space, where man cannot yet travel. Their instruments and cameras observe and record information about distant worlds and radio pictures and measurements back to Earth. The picture shows the most successful of all space probes so far, the American built Voyager. Two Voyager probes were launched which sent back fantastic pictures of the giant planets Jupiter and Saturn.

Below: This curious beetle-like craft is an experimental robot vessel designed to locate and retrieve objects under water. When working, it supports itself on legs, while its arms carry out the necessary tasks. It is a development of the type of manned submersible craft now being used in offshore oil fields.

The great advantage of robots over human workers is that they can work non-stop for long periods. They never get tired, and always work with the same accuracy. They can also work in conditions that humans could not bear, where it is very hot, very noisy, or where there are dangerous rays. Last but not least, as more robots are built, their cost will come down. Human labor costs, on the other hand, are continually rising.

Although robots are rapidly taking over many jobs in industry, they seem a long way from taking over in the home. The problem is that it would take a very complex and costly robot to perform half the tasks involved in housework.

Index